Red Africa

About Salvage Editions

Salvage Editions is a collaboration between Verso Books and the journal *Salvage*. Edited by the Salvage Collective, some of the books extend and develop arguments initially published in *Salvage*, others are entirely new. As with all *Salvage*'s publishing, Salvage Editions intervenes in the key theoretical and political questions thrown up by our moment in ways both politically incisive and stylistically ambitious and engaged. Put simply, the Salvage Collective does not believe that radical writing should not also strive for beauty.

Since 2015, *Salvage* has been publishing essays, poetry, fiction and visual art in its print edition, currently published twice a year. In 2020, the Salvage Collective began the Salvage Editions series as well as a live online events series in collaboration with Haymarket Books called Salvage Live.

Over the years and issues, a cluster of concerns has emerged as core to *Salvage*'s project, including the global political economy; modern political subjectivity; the social industries; sexuality, race and identity; and eco-socialism.

For more on *Salvage*, including information about subscribing, please go to salvage.zone.

Red Africa

Reclaiming Revolutionary
Black Politics

Kevin Ochieng Okoth

VERSO
London • New York

First published by Verso 2023
© Kevin Ochieng Okoth 2023

1 3 5 7 9 10 8 6 4 2

Verso
UK: 6 Meard Street, London W1F 0EG
US: 388 Atlantic Avenue, Brooklyn, NY 11217
versobooks.com

Verso is the imprint of New Left Books

ISBN-13: 978-1-83976-737-1
ISBN-13: 978-1-83976-738-8 (UK EBK)
ISBN-13: 978-1-83976-739-5 (US EBK)

British Library Cataloguing in Publication Data
A catalogue record for this book is available from the British Library

Library of Congress Cataloging-in-Publication Data

Names: Okoth, Kevin Ochieng, author.
Title: Red Africa : reclaiming revolutionary Black politics / Kevin Ochieng
  Okoth.
Other titles: Salvage editions.
Description: London ; New York : Verso, 2023. | Series: Salvage editions |
  Includes bibliographical references.
Identifiers: LCCN 2023017166 (print) | LCCN 2023017167 (ebook) | ISBN
  9781839767371 (trade paperback) | ISBN 9781839767395 (ebook)
Subjects: LCSH: Decolonization—Africa. | Self-determination,
  National—Africa. | Communism—Africa. | Africa—Politics and
  government—1960-
Classification: LCC DT30.5 .O366 2023 (print)
| LCC DT30.5 (ebook) | DDC
  320.96—dc23/eng/20230411
LC record available at https://lccn.loc.gov/2023017166
LC ebook record available at https://lccn.loc.gov/2023017167

Typeset in Sabon by Hewer Text UK Ltd, Edinburgh
Printed and bound by CPI Group (UK) Ltd, Croydon CR0 4YY

Contents

Preface

The RhodesMustFall protests, which erupted in universities across South Africa in 2015, brought mainstream attention to debates about 'decolonising' education. Though the protests had started with a call to remove the statue of Cecil Rhodes from the University of Cape Town campus, they soon transformed into a wider movement that questioned how colonialism had shaped education policy in South Africa. Black students demanded answers: Why did the curriculum not reflect the diversity of the student body? Why was the university still institutionally racist, despite the end of apartheid in the early 1990s? And why were fees so high that university education was out of reach for most Black South Africans?[1]

Their frustrations with the unfinished project of decolonisation resonated with me; after all, South Africa had never truly become the 'rainbow nation' it claimed to be. Yet one thing struck me as odd: some activists embraced the language of 'Afro-pessimism', which claimed that there were irreconcilable differences between Black people and non-Black people of colour.[2] Wasn't this a departure from the Black Consciousness philosophy of the movement's hero, Steve Biko, who had called for a coalition of 'African', 'Indian' and 'Coloured' South Africans in the struggle against apartheid?[3]

This clearly wasn't the Afro-pessimism I was familiar with. For decades, Afro-pessimism referred to the negative coverage of Africa in Western news media, especially the reporting on the region as suffering from arrested development. This discourse, loosely united by an emphasis on the desperation of Africa – and exemplified by the scandalous 2000 *Economist* cover story describing the continent as 'hopeless' – provided the rationale for the imperialist economic policies of the International Monetary Fund (IMF) and the World Bank's structural adjustment programmes.[4] The narrative was that Africa is one big, tragic mess: corruption, cronyism and ethnic conflict were thought to govern politics and other daily experiences. For the editors of the *Economist*, the reasons for Africa's persistent crises were clear: 'These acts are not exclusively African . . . but African societies, for reasons buried in their cultures, seem especially susceptible to them.'[5] In short, crisis was endemic. The looting of Africa by imperialism supposedly had little to do with it.

A long time has passed since the *Economist* published this cover story, but how much has really changed? Today, Afro-pessimist narratives have again come to the fore, most recently in news lamenting the return of the military coup 'in Africa'.[6] The claim is, again, that this is somehow the natural outcome of an 'African' way of doing politics. But the repetition of simplistic prejudices does not make them any truer. The crisis of postcolonial African states cannot simply be explained away by pointing to a cultural deficiency on the part of sub-Saharan or

Black Africans. Afro-pessimism provides the grand narrative to justify the continued exploitation of the continent's people and resources by obscuring imperialist practices that undermine the sovereignty of African states. Moreover, it prevents us from better understanding the challenges or solutions to political problems in postcolonial African countries. This is, of course, deliberate. Is there any better way to mask imperialism's hold over the continent?

When the term Afro-pessimism recently began appearing in books, journal articles and, curiously, on activist social media, referring to an entirely different discourse, I was admittedly confused. But I was curious, too. Where had this new Afro-pessimism come from? Did it have anything to do with the old Afro-pessimism? Did it have anything to do with Africa at all? As it turned out, the new Afro-pessimism (from now on AP 2.0) has nothing to do with knotty questions about postcolonial African politics.[7] AP 2.0 is a highly theoretical discourse which has tried to make sense of the persistent violence and discrimination against Black people in the United States despite the achievements of the Civil Rights era. But, true to its name, it shares none of that era's optimism. For AP 2.0, I soon found out, anti-Black racism is not historical or contingent; that is, it cannot be overcome by addressing the concerns of Black people in the political sphere. Blackness, for AP 2.0, is an eternal condition that precludes Black people's participation in politics and condemns them to a life of 'social death'.

This attitude of despair seemed to me to reflect the same essentialist prejudices as the discourse that had lent AP 2.0 its name. AP 2.0, too, suggested that there was something inherently un-modern about Blackness. For AP 2.0, Africa was simply the place from where enslaved Black people had been shipped off to the Americas, only to be dehumanised on their way to the plantations via the Middle Passage. By reducing an entire continent's history to a singular traumatic event, AP 2.0 was echoing the same fantastical view of Africa – which lets the continent fade into the background and offers it up as a blank slate on which to imprint our own narratives, myths and beliefs – which has so often prevented us from better understanding its realities. But how could AP 2.0 claim that Black people, and by extension Black Africans, could do nothing to resist their oppression? Hadn't Black people from all over the continent contributed to the historical project of national liberation?

While the thrust of AP 2.0 was understandable considering the seemingly endless cycle of police violence against Black people in the United States, it had nothing to offer activists working, for example, towards police abolition on the ground. This supposedly radical discourse precluded the very idea of a politics that might enable us to transform social relations and imagine a different, better world. Therefore, what was at stake in the debate, I thought, was the very possibility of a revolutionary Black politics. There was also the matter of the erasure of a political tradition of national liberation Marxism, which had produced some of the most radical political thought in the twentieth century. As I read and discussed AP 2.0's key thinkers, I kept on encountering the claim that Marxism had nothing to offer Black people, or that it was inherently Eurocentric and should therefore be discarded. This claim is, of course, both theoretically and historically false. Yet somehow Black activists and scholars had come to accept it as true.

The erasure of anti-colonial Marxism in Africa didn't begin and end with AP 2.0. I could discern a similar turn away from the politics of national liberation *and* Marxism in contemporary debates about 'decolonising'. Decolonial studies, which lends discourses on decolonising the museum or universities its theoretical framework, claimed that Marxism is Eurocentric, too. Moreover, its proponents argued that the politics of national liberation were destined to fail because of their fetishisation of the nation-state. But the turn away from decolonisation, understood as transforming a 'colony into a self-governing entity with its political and economic fortunes under its own direction', creates a distance between current debates and the historical event itself.[8] Without this historical reference point, the debate on decolonising would lose sight of what the object of its discontent is. What did 'decolonising' even mean if it was applied without reference to national liberation? And what resources did it offer to those fighting against imperialism in the global south?

The following chapters avoid the pitfalls of idealist historiography which present the decline of national liberation as pre-programmed. *Red Africa* challenges common misconceptions about national liberation by developing a distinctly anti-colonial and Black-revolutionary historiographic perspective – akin to what Walter Rodney has called the 'view from the Third World' – which links the contradictions of postcolonial sovereignty with universal questions about socialist strategy, and allows us to place anti-colonial Marxism within its proper historical and theoretical context. In doing so, this book seeks to address an impasse in anti-imperialist politics: the separation between decolonisation, or Black radicalism, and Marxism.[9] This separation has stopped us from fully grasping the emancipatory potential of national liberation Marxism in Africa. The horizon of these politics was never limited to the nation-building projects of the continent's post-independence governments.

The phrase 'Red Africa' is used to distinguish a revolutionary anti-colonial tradition from the reformist politics of African socialism. While African socialists sought to distance themselves from Marxism and argued for a 'third way' socialism rooted in 'traditional African culture', the intellectual and political tradition discussed below showed that Marxism and Black radicalism were not incompatible. 'Red Africa' does not simply refer to those national liberation movements who collaborated closely with China or the Soviet Union.[10] Instead, it points to a tradition whose activism envisioned a different postcolonial future than the one that has come to pass. The book follows David Scott in trying to make sense of 'our present after the collapse of the social and political hopes that went into the anticolonial imagining and postcolonial making of national sovereignties'.[11] I hope to show that the politics of Red Africa have not been exhausted, and that anti-colonial futures might yet be imagined anew.

This is not simply an exercise in nostalgia or a longing for a time when revolutionary change seemed possible. Rather, it is a political project that hopes to salvage what remains of the tradition of Red Africa – which has been betrayed, violently suppressed, or erased – and to build from it a Black revolutionary politics. It is, in short, an attempt at *Salvage*-Marxism: a communism of the ruins which reclaims the legacy of national liberation. We still have a lot to learn from the politics of Eduardo Mondlane, Amílcar Cabral, Walter Rodney and Andrée Blouin. We might yet build something new from their political thought, something which clings on to the utopian promise of freedom and refuses to let go.

Decolonisation and the Decline of the 'Bandung Spirit'

In April 1955, delegates from twenty-nine Asian and African countries assembled in Bandung, Indonesia, for the first ever Afro-Asian Conference. Indonesia had declared its independence from the Dutch only a few years earlier, and its president Sukarno was eager to assert the country's sovereignty on a world-political stage. But the Bandung conference was more than just a celebration of Indonesian independence. For the first time, nations from the global south could meet and discuss their shared vision for a post-imperial world order without interference from the West.[1] Earlier attempts at Afro-Asian solidarity had been complicated by racism, and the nationalist leaders at Bandung vowed to not let this happen again. Instead, they resolved to make the basis of their shared politics the rejection of colonialism and imperialism, not racial or cultural similarities.[2] In his report from Bandung, later published as *The Color Curtain*, the novelist Richard Wright praised the conference as 'a meeting of almost all of the human race living in the geopolitical center of gravity of earth'.[3] This was, of course, hyperbole, but Wright had a point:

an estimated 1.5 billion people, around half of the world's population at the time, were represented at Bandung. The 'Bandung spirit', which expressed a feeling of Third World solidarity and a duty of mutual support, set the stage for an ever-closer union of African and Asian nations. And while the policy conclusions outlined in the conference communiqué remained vague, Bandung imprinted the idea of the Third World in the global political imaginary.

In the early post-war years, the intensification of Cold War competition had forced nations in the global south to align themselves with either the United States or the Soviet Union. But Bandung sent a clear message to the two superpowers: Third World nationalists had their own political ideology which could not be reduced to either capitalism or Soviet-style communism. By 1961, when the Non-Aligned Movement was formally established in Belgrade, Serbia, the Bandung spirit had captured the imagination not only of anti-colonial nationalists from Asia and Africa, but of 120 nations from across the world who refused to enter multilateral agreements with the West or military pacts with the USSR.[4] Founded by Sukarno, Josip Broz Tito of Yugoslavia, Kwame Nkrumah of Ghana, Jawaharlal Nehru of India and Gamal Abdel Nasser of Egypt, the Non-Aligned Movement gave a political voice to nations who had been relegated to secondary status in the international arena of the Cold War.[5] But nonalignment did not mean that radical nationalists rejected socialism as a political ideology. The most explicitly leftist organisation that grew out of the Bandung moment was the Organization of Solidarity with the People of Asia, Africa and Latin America (OSPAAAL), founded in Havana following the Tricontinental Conference in 1966, which imbued Third World nationalism with an explicitly socialist ideology. OSPAAAL sought to give institutional form to what, according to Fidel Castro, had been a 'great feast of international solidarity'.[6] Under Cuban leadership, OSPAAAL went beyond Bandung's vague expressions of a Third Worldist 'spirit' by proposing concrete measures for political, economic and military collaboration.

The rise of Third Worldism coincided with a flourishing of Pan-Africanism and Black internationalist politics. The All-African Peoples' Conference (AAPC), which took place in Accra, Ghana, in December 1958, was in the Bandung spirit, but its agenda directly addressed the concerns of anti-colonial and Black activists from Africa and its diaspora. Bandung's focus on racism and culture appealed to Black activists, but the lack of African nations in attendance had sparked a desire for a different kind of conference. The AAPC was organised by the Pan-Africanist George Padmore, whom Nkrumah had appointed as his new advisor on African affairs. Padmore shared Nkrumah's political vision and recognised how important anti-colonial nationalisms and anti-racist struggles were to the success of a world revolution.[7] Between 1919 and 1945, Black radicals like W.E.B. Du Bois and Padmore had organised a series of Pan-African conferences in Paris, Brussels, London, New York and Manchester. But the AAPC finally brought Pan-Africanism to the continent. Ghana had achieved independence from British colonial rule in March 1957, and Nkrumah hoped that other African countries would soon follow suit. Under the guidance of Padmore, Ghana's capital became a sanctuary for exiled anti-colonial nationalists; here they could discuss the question of decolonisation without fear of censorship or repression. But Black radicals from the metropole also found a political home in Accra, which developed into a new hub of Black internationalism.[8]

By 1975, however, the Bandung era was coming to an end. But what caused the decline of a politics which, only two decades earlier, promised to liberate the Third World from imperialism?[9] Beginning with the US-sponsored 1973 coup d'état in Chile, which deposed Salvador Allende's socialist government and enabled Augusto Pinochet's rise to power, Washington started to 'promote' the implementation of neoliberal economic doctrine across the global south. The 1973–74 oil crisis hit non-petroleum-exporting countries in the global south especially hard. Faced with tough budgetary constraints and ballooning debt, they were forced to look to international financial institutions to cover their government spending. But with the loans came conditions. Though the initial cause of the debt crisis was obvious – the overreliance of formerly colonised nations on the export of primary commodities, whose prices they couldn't control – the structural adjustment programmes (SAPs) that were imposed on them did little to alleviate such pressures. Instead, the economies of poorer nations were restructured according to the dictates of US-controlled 'international' institutions like the International Monetary Fund (IMF) and the World Bank. 'The IMF', writes Vijay Prashad, 'arrived with one prescription to fit all ailments': austerity. A tightening in the monetary supply, high interest rates, reduced government spending, lower wages and the scrapping of government subsidies all meant that it was increasingly difficult to implement a domestic developmental agenda. Debt repayment soon took priority over social spending – and the working people of the poorer nations were made to suffer for the acquiescence of their elites.[10]

With few exceptions, the national bourgeoisies, once the leaders of national liberation, had been co-opted, deposed or assassinated by the following decade. A new elite was formed which increasingly distanced itself from the political aspirations of the majority of the population. The Egyptian economist Samir Amin suggested that Bandung nations were naive to believe that the international order was willing to accommodate the reasonable demands of these new national bourgeois projects.[11] Their anti-colonial nationalism was antithetical to the aims of neoliberalism, which sought to bring a minimalist version of national sovereignty in line with the principles of a new global economic order designed to strengthen imperialism's hold over the Third World. As a political and ideological project, neoliberalism didn't merely restate the principles of libertarian free market ideology; rather, it encouraged states to develop multilateral institutions which could 'insulate' free market actors from democratic pressures that interfered with their profit-making motives. Far from displacing states in the international order, neoliberalism worked 'with and through [the state] to ensure the proper functioning of the whole'.[12] In short, international financial institutions and multinational companies undermined the state's 'economic "self-determination" while maintaining its role of domination and regulation with respect to the relations of production'.[13]

To free multinational companies from the constraints of democratic accountability, Western governments and international organisations supported, or at the very least tolerated, regimes across the global south that were resolutely anti-democratic in nature. Ironically, foreign intervention to secure regime change in 'hostile' nations was carried out under the guise of 'promoting democracy'. The neo-colonial (or comprador) elite often drew its legitimacy from a watered-down nationalism that had little to do with the radical nationalism of the Bandung era. The idea of social cohesion based on racial, cultural or ethnic commonalities returned to the forefront of politics, as anti-imperialist solidarity, which had provided the ideological scaffolding for the Third World project, faded into the background. In most cases, postcolonial realities, marked by political repression, massive debt increases, rising inequality and violent conflict, offered little respite for working people in the Third World. Yet this was not the only outcome of national liberation. East Asia, for example, embarked on a process of rapid capitalist development, which allowed countries like South Korea and Taiwan to assert themselves on the international stage (though these political projects were also anti-democratic). China, too, ascended to the status of a global power. Moreover, the collapse of the Portuguese empire in Africa, which brought leftist parties to power in Guinea-Bissau, Cape Verde, Mozambique and Angola, and the defeat of US imperialism in Vietnam in the mid-1970s, showed that socialism and anti-imperialism still appealed to radical nationalist movements. But for much of the global south, the utopia promised by Bandung, the Non-Aligned Movement, and the Tricontinental conference proved elusive.[14]

The triumph of neoliberalism also signalled the end of a fruitful period of Black internationalism. In the early to mid-twentieth century, Black radicals in the United States had treated anti-racism and anti-imperialism as part of the same political struggle. 'Before the Negroes of the Western world can play an effective part [in the world revolution]', wrote the Harlem radical Hubert Harrison in 1920, 'they must first acquaint themselves with what is taking place in the larger world whose millions are in motion.'[15] Shortly before his assassination in February 1965, Malcolm X, long an advocate of a militant (and parochial) Black nationalism, returned from a trip to Africa convinced that Black people in the United States should also be invested in the anti-colonial struggle in Africa. But these Black internationalist or Pan-African politics were often influenced by close relationships that Black radicals forged with nationalist leaders in the Third World. Towards the end of the twentieth century, there weren't many radical nationalist leaders or projects left to inspire Black radical politics in the United States. The assassination of Patrice Lumumba in 1961, orchestrated by the CIA and the Belgian government, and the CIA-sponsored coup that brought down Nkrumah's government, dealt a particularly harsh blow to Black internationalism. Even Ghana and the Democratic Republic of Congo, once beacons of the Black radical imagination, had become US-backed military regimes.

Seemingly not content with the demise of Third Worldist projects that challenged its rule, neoliberalism reshaped the discourse on decolonisation, too. One need only consider contemporary debates on decolonising the museums, art galleries and universities to get a better sense of how the terrain of 'decolonisation' has shifted from a focus on the critique of political economy to the more abstract question of decolonising knowledge(s).[16]

The recent focus on epistemic, symbolic or cultural concerns of decolonisation can largely be attributed to the Decolonial Studies (DS) school spearheaded by the Argentinian linguist Walter Mignolo, which has re-conceptualised decolonisation as a purely academic and intellectual issue. While the discourse encompasses multiple strands of writing on colonialism and epistemology, DS scholars share a common set of theoretical positions, including Enrique Dussel's anti-universalism, Mignolo's geopolitics of knowledge, Immanuel Wallerstein's world-systems theory, and Sandra Harding's standpoint theory, an epistemic approach which argues that research must begin with the perspectives of the most oppressed and marginalised, since they are socially situated in a way that gives them an advantage in gaining certain forms of knowledge. Most importantly, however, DS builds on the concept of the coloniality of power first articulated by Aníbal Quijano to describe a 'matrix of power that produces racial and gender hierarchies on the global and local level, functioning alongside capital to maintain a modern regime of exploitation and domination'.[17]

For Quijano, coloniality is a mode of power that has its roots in two historical processes: the codification of difference (i.e., superiority/inferiority) in the idea of race, and the establishment of new modes of control which made labour and resources available for capitalist accumulation. Such formulations are, of course, nothing new. But it is Quijano's linking of modernity and coloniality in a singular matrix that constitutes his major contribution. What this matrix enables us to see is that coloniality is the other – dark – side of modernity, the inevitable outcome of an epistemological frame that enables the colonial project to survive in reconstituted forms. Mignolo and other DS scholars supposedly offer a way out of the oppressive bind of Quijano's modernity/coloniality matrix. As Mignolo explains in *On Decoloniality*:

> If there is no modernity without coloniality, if coloniality is constitutive of modernity, if the '/' [in the triad modernity/coloniality/decoloniality] divides and connects, then decoloniality proposes the undoing of modernity. That is, decoloniality implies demodernity. At the same time, modernity/coloniality engender decoloniality. So there would be no decoloniality – and decoloniality would not be necessary – if modernity/coloniality had not created the need to delink from the rhetoric of modernity and the logic of coloniality.[18]

DS proposes new ways of 'thinking, sensing, believing, doing, and living' that delink from the Eurocentric knowledge production of modernity. Its aim, then, is to enable a reconstitution of knowledge based on 'epistemic pluriversality': the coexisting epistemologies and practices of the multiple worlds that the cultural and linguistic Other inhabits. In doing so, they are pushing back against modernity, which relies on a philosophical anthropology that, to borrow a phrase from Sylvia Wynter, overrepresents European man as if it were the Human itself, and subjugates those who have been categorised as subhuman according to colonial logics.

There is a tension between the emancipatory aims to which DS pledges allegiance, the theoretical framework it proposes, and its proponents' positionality in the international (and intellectual) division of labour. What are the implications for anti-imperialist struggle in the global south if those at the forefront of challenging the Eurocentricity of knowledge production are based in the resource-hoarding universities of the global north (and especially in the United States)? Is there not a danger here of reproducing precisely the kind of epistemic coloniality from which we are trying to delink? And what are we to make of DS' reliance on a deferential version of standpoint theory, whose narrow focus on 'spokespeople from marginalised groups' could prevent us from centring those voices whose exclusion DS claims to be fighting against? As Olúfẹ́mi O. Táíwò explains, 'The concept of elite capture originated in the study of developing countries to describe the way socially advantaged people tend to gain control over financial benefits, especially foreign aid, meant for others'. But 'elite capture' can also be used to describe 'how political projects can be hijacked in principle or in effect by the well positioned and resourced'.[19] There is, perhaps, an analogy to be made between certain types of scholars in the neoliberal university and the neocolonial elites; both enable the reproduction of a system that ensures the continued exploitation of the very people they claim to represent.

Táíwò is not the only one concerned with elite capture. In 'Reflection on the Practices and Discourses of Decolonisation', a forcefully argued critique of DS, the Bolivian Anarcho-feminist Silvia Rivera Cusicanqui takes aim at a Latin American intelligentsia that strikes post-modern and even post-colonial poses, and to the US academy and its followers who built pyramidal structures of power and symbolic capital – baseless pyramids that vertically blind certain Latin American universities – and form clientilist networks with indigenous and black intellectuals.[20]

These intellectuals, she argues, reproduce a 'conditional inclusion' – a sort of 'second-class citizenship that moulds subaltern imaginaries and identities into the role of ornaments through which the anonymous masses play out the theatricality of their own identity'. By reducing Indigenous peoples to the marginal status of minorities, 'noble savages' or 'guardians of nature', scholars like Mignolo and Catherine Walsh effectively exclude them from modernity and the crucial struggles that are waged within it. Cusicanqui accuses Mignolo of building a 'small empire within an empire' – a formation that perpetuates coloniality in Latin America by 'enthroning' decolonisation in the academy.[21] Through the appropriation and depoliticisation of the work of radical Indigenous scholarship, like that of Cusicanqui herself, Mignolo marginalises these scholars and activists from the very debates that they themselves started and are still engaged in. This, in turn, limits the imaginative power and emancipatory potential of their discourse on 'decolonisation'.

Decolonial Studies' concept of delinking does not correspond to the Bandung-era demand, elaborated theoretically by Amin, that nations in the global south should economically and politically delink from imperialism. Rather, delinking here takes place exclusively on an epistemic level. This is because, Mignolo and his frequent collaborator Walsh argue, decoloniality delinks from the knowledge of political theory, political economy and the corresponding subject formation these knowledges entail.[22] DS makes a sharp distinction between colonialism as it is commonly understood and the more abstract phenomenon of *coloniality*. While colonialism simply refers to a political and economic relation in which 'the sovereignty of a nation or a people rests on the power of another nation', coloniality refers instead to the underlying 'patterns of power' – in the spheres of knowledge production or culture, for example – that have survived beyond the official end of colonial domination.[23] For Mignolo and Walsh, the national liberation movements of the Bandung era were engaged in 'dewesternisation'; that is, they were simply trying to fight coloniality on its own terms (those of the nation-state), thus failing to challenge the 'epistemic empire' that colonialism created. Decoloniality, on the other hand, is not a state-led project, but emerges from 'people organizing themselves in their local histories'.[24] Theirs, they argue, is the only true decolonising praxis.

In her 1993 essay 'Public Enemies and Private Intellectuals', Ruth Wilson Gilmore takes issue with three approaches to scholarship that have shaped how marginalised academics present themselves in the neoliberal university. Gilmore groups these approaches together under the banner of 'oppositional studies', which includes overlapping approaches such as 'individual careerism', 'romantic particularism' and 'luxury production'. She defines romantic particularism as the tendency to uncritically celebrate the essential 'authenticity' of epistemologies and cultures that have been suppressed by colonialism and imperialism. Luxury production, on the other hand, refers the relatively comfortable site (i.e., the university) from which these scholars produce 'oppositional' knowledge. For Gilmore, the final tendency, individual careerism, 'assigns primary importance to the fact – and survival – of oppositional studies within the intellectual and social structures of the university'.[25] To this end, scholars become obsessed with the idea of being the first to coin a theoretical concept or the most knowledgeable about a new oppositional object – a performance, text or theory, for example. All three tendencies lead oppositional scholars to distance themselves from broader social struggles taking place outside of the university, while they continue to derive their academic credibility from a close identification with precisely these struggles.

Like Decolonial Studies, postcolonial studies, too, seems to have a bone to pick with anti-colonial nationalisms. Though he takes issue with its theorisation of multiplicity as difference (i.e., romantic particularism), Achille Mbembe, one of the foremost African thinkers of the twenty-first century, shares with DS a distrust for the politics of national liberation, especially when aligned closely with Marxism.[26] For Mbembe, the African encounter with Marxism and nationalism resulted in a formation he calls 'Afro-radicalism'. (Conflicting discourses such as Négritude, African socialism and Afro-Marxism, or what I call 'Red Africa', are here treated as part of the same episteme, but more on that later.) Afro-radicalism split history into three major events – slavery, colonialism and apartheid – which led the African self to become 'alienated from itself'.[27] It suggested that Africans must unite around these three events to form political identities that enable them to finally 'know themselves, to recapture their destiny (sovereignty), and to belong to themselves in the world (autonomy)'.[28] But Afro-radicalism remained stuck between voluntarism and victimisation, both of which prevented Africans from truly understanding their subjectivity (it also retreated into a fetishisation of difference by emphasising Africa's cultural uniqueness). Because its philosophical foundations were too weak, Mbembe concludes, Afro-radicalism failed to re-fashion or liberate the African subject. Instead, this mode of critique resulted in political projects characterised by their mechanistic vision of history, 'the fetishization of state power, the disqualification of liberal democracy, and the populist and authoritarian dream of mass society'.[29] Marxism and nationalism, then, have little to offer Africans today; they are, in Mbembe's words, 'hollow constructs of dead elements'.

This portrait of national liberation leaves a lot to be desired. Like DS, Mbembe entirely ignores the fact that the horizon of national liberation *did* extend beyond the construct of the nation-state or the fetishisation of cultural difference.[30] Laying claim to an independent nation-state was never an end in itself but a tragic necessity – one which does not necessarily limit the aspirations of national liberation.[31] When we consider what Adom Getachew calls the 'worldmaking aspirations' of anti-colonial nationalisms, we begin to understand 'the specificity of the questions and contradictions' that animated their politics.[32] While one can agree with Michael Hardt and Antonio Negri that the nation-state is a 'poisoned gift of national liberation', and that there are, of course, problems with the state form, one cannot chastise movements struggling for control over it.[33] The point, then, is not to dismiss anti-colonial movements that have fought for an independent nation-state, but to suggest that the struggle cannot end there. But Mbembe and DS elevate the purity of the decolonial project above all else, seemingly ignoring the constraints of actually existing postcolonialism in actually existing capitalist modernity. The question of how it is possible to do without the state in a capitalist system of nation-states is never addressed.

Freedom, as articulated by the national liberation movements, was based on the right to self-determination – a political question concerning the democratic rights of oppressed nations. Two different interpretations of self-determination emerged in the early twentieth century: Woodrow Wilson's call for a 'free, open minded, and absolutely impartial adjustment of all colonial claims' at the Paris Peace Conference in 1919, and the Bolshevik conception of the right to self-determination.[34] For Lenin, self-determination was a revolutionary principle which could break apart the reactionary empires of Europe. Wilson, on the other hand, thought self-determination would achieve precisely the opposite: to protect an existing imperial order against radical challenges like the Mexican or Russian revolutions.[35] While the Bolshevik conception of self-determination gave colonised peoples the language to challenge the existing international order and call for a radical break with the colonial past, the Wilsonian moment was a counterrevolutionary episode.[36] Wilson's declaration 'excised the Bolshevik right to self-determination and repurposed the principle to preserve racial hierarchy' in the new international order, making it entirely 'compatible with imperial rule'.[37] Of course, colonised peoples felt they had been short-changed. While such disappointment would eventually lead to the emergence of early anti-colonial nationalisms in Asia and the Middle East, the Wilsonian moment severely limited the arena in which colonised peoples could make their 'world-making' claims.

The post-Wilsonian order still governs international politics, though American imperialism is not as unrestrained as it once was (the rise of China, for example, has complicated its hegemonic designs). We now find ourselves at an impasse. If the postcolonial present is characterised by the failure of national liberation to re-imagine the international order, what might take its place? To establish a new mode of anti-imperialist politics, I propose that we must do four things (though the list offered here is by no means exhaustive). First, we must re-assess the victories and failures of national liberation Marxism to recover what remains of its vision of a post-imperialist world. Second, we must return to the critique of political economy to determine how poorer nations in the global south might overcome their peripheral integration into the capitalist world economy.[38] Third, we must refuse the temptation to retreat into romantic particularism. Instead, we should embrace historical materialism as a method for better understanding how capitalism governs through hierarchy and difference. And finally, we must again forge crucial anti-imperialist solidarities between revolutionary struggles in the global north and south. But this also requires work within the confines of institutions like the neoliberal university, which has sought to isolate scholars from social struggles on the ground. Only then can we begin to form a new theory and practice of decolonisation which is grounded in a tradition of revolutionary anti-imperialism. The following chapters hope to contribute to this endeavour.

2

From Black Studies to Afro-pessimism: The Making of an Anti-politics

In May 1954, the US Supreme Court overturned legally mandated segregation in public schools. *Brown v. Board of Education*, which declared that racial segregation was in breach of the US constitution, was a landmark achievement of the Civil Rights era. But it didn't transform the American educational system as Black activists had hoped: some southern cities outright rejected desegregation, choosing instead to encourage white students to attend segregated private academies, which fell outside of the remit of the Supreme Court ruling. For the next decade, schools in Black areas remained de facto segregated and underfunded; some were forced to close their doors entirely.

Brown v. Board of Education showed that the legalistic achievements of the Civil Rights era couldn't guarantee improved educational opportunities for Black people in the United States. When Black students entered historically white colleges and universities (HWCU) after desegregation, they found that they were still discriminated against, marginalised from campus life or alienated by the Eurocentric curriculum that was being taught. Historically

Black colleges and universities (HBCU), on the other hand, retained their mostly white faculty or hired conservative Black academics. 'The problems that needed to be addressed', writes Stanley Crouch in his introduction to Harold Cruse's *The Crisis of the Negro Intellectual*, 'were seen as calling for something other than integrationist reform.'[1] What was required, then, was nothing short of revolutionary change in the core institutions of the United States.

The Black Campus Movement, as a wave of student protests between 1965 and 1975 is often referred to, sought to revolutionise higher education in the United States. Students at more than a thousand colleges and universities 'disrupted higher education in almost every area of the nation – the Midwest in Illinois and Wisconsin; the Northeast in New York; the Upper South in North Carolina; the deep South in Mississippi; the West Coast in the Bay Area'.[2] Like Cruse, student activists felt that Civil Rights–era intellectuals had not been radical enough. One of the main demands of the Black student protests that spread across US campuses in the mid-1960s was the creation of Black studies programmes, which would form a new kind of activist-intellectual that was more closely connected to the histories and struggles of the Black masses. During the protests, student activists disrupted classes or occupied buildings to teach Black studies and engage in critical pedagogy. At Duke, for example, Black students took over the university's central records section and renamed it the Malcolm X Liberation School. Led by the community activist Howard Fuller, the school became a hub for Black students who had been expelled by other universities during the protests. The curriculum was inspired by Pan-Africanist ideology, and offered instruction in African languages like Yoruba, Hausa and Swahili, alongside technical training that would enable students to contribute to the liberation of Black people in Africa and its diaspora.[3]

In 1969, the activist-scholars Vincent Harding, Stephen Henderson (both faculty at historically Black colleges) and William Strickland set up the Institute of the Black World (IBW), an organisation which promoted critical research into political ideologies that might be of use to the Black struggle (they also collected data on the development of Black studies programmes across the country). Their interdisciplinary methodology hoped to move beyond racial integration by combining Marxism, Black nationalism and Pan-Africanism to address specific issues that affected Black communities.[4] The initial funds for the project were made available by the Martin Luther King Jr. Center for Nonviolent Social Change, established in 1968, shortly after his assassination. The IBW was initially on good terms with the King Center, but the relationship soon deteriorated, and the institute was left without funding. While the King Center adopted a liberal anti-racism as its official position, the IBW invited Black Power activists like Stokely Carmichael (later Kwame Ture), whom many considered 'the complete antithesis of King and his legacy of nonviolence', to speak at the institute.[5] Though members of the IBW included prominent Black scholar-activists like C.L.R. James, Sylvia Wynter and Walter Rodney, the anthropologist and choreographer Katherine Dunham, and the Nigerian novelist Chinua Achebe, Harding and his colleagues struggled to find alternative funding. Unable to make ends meet, many of the institute's associates returned to teaching at various universities across the country.[6]

By the late sixties, the Bandung spirit of Third Worldism had reached American campuses. At the University of California, Berkeley, and San Francisco State University, where the idea of Black studies had first emerged in 1966, students formed the Third World Liberation Front (TWLF), an anti-imperialist alliance of student organisations like the Black Students Union; the Mexican Student Confederation; the Philippine American Collegiate Endeavour (PACE); La Raza; the Native Students Union; and the Asian-American Political Alliance. The strikes organised by the TWLF at San Francisco State in 1968–69 were the longest student strikes in US history, and resulted in the establishment of the first-ever department of ethnic studies.[7] By drawing parallels between the struggles of oppressed minorities on campus with those of national liberation movements in the Third World, student activists were building solidarities that projected their politics beyond the national context.[8] At the same time, they were rejecting the integrationist advances of the US state which, as Lisa Lowe explains in *Immigrant Acts*, demanded that they 'forget' the histories of imperialism, war and neo-colonialism that had destroyed their home countries if they wanted to access citizenship.[9] But despite such attempts at refashioning immigrant groups as national subjects, their presence in the country was a constant reminder of the violence of US imperialism. Ethnic studies, as imagined by the TWLF, would finally make this implicit critique of US power explicit by giving Third World peoples their own programme of study, which 'would serve their communities, retrieve their historical legacy, and advance social change'.[10] Most importantly, however, the programme would be under the control of marginalised groups themselves. They too demanded self-determination.

There were, of course, tense debates about the ideological direction of the campus movement. In *The Black Revolution on Campus*, Martha Biondi recalls a debate between Marxist-Leninists, Pan-Africanists and Black nationalists at a meeting of the African Heritage Studies Association at Wayne State University in Detroit.[11] The meeting led to a clash between the Marxists and the Black nationalists, who disagreed on whether their enemy was simply racism in the US or the larger system of capitalist imperialism. Eventually the Black nationalists gained the upper hand in the debate, sidelining the activists who hoped to build links with anti-colonial and anti-imperialist movements in Africa – especially the revolutionary 'struggles against white settler regimes in South Africa and Zimbabwe and Portuguese colonial rule in Angola, Guinea-Bissau, and Mozambique'. Inspired by anti-colonial Marxism, activists like Fuller (later Owusu Sadukai), who had travelled to Mozambique and 'returned with a new perspective on the character of imperialism' following several 'encounters with liberation leaders and struggles', attempted to combat Black anti-communism in the US. Such efforts led many Black radical organisations to adopt Maoism or Marxist-Leninism, political programmes that were resolutely anti-imperialist. But the radicalisation of the movement took place mainly outside of the university: as Biondi explains, it was 'the black revolution off-campus'.[12]

On campus, however, the movement quickly disintegrated. The late sixties and early seventies were a time of intense police and government repression, which made organising difficult for radical student activists. In

'Decorative Beasts', a short essay on academia's relationship to marginalised scholars, Ruth Wilson Gilmore remembers her cousin John Huggins and his comrade Alprentice Carter, both members of the Black Panther Party, who were murdered at the University of California, Los Angeles, in January 1969.[13] Their assassination was a deliberate move by the US State to silence Black studies activists who called 'for a curriculum that centered on race and capitalism as inseparable elements of US and global analysis'. Moreover, they had dared to question the direction of Black studies, which was losing touch with its original mission. Reformist demands for the institutionalisation of Black studies as African American studies (without the revolutionary transformation of higher education, of course) replaced activist Black studies, as universities and colleges hired Black academics in a drive to 'diversify' their faculties.[14] The discipline, Black studies or African American studies, soon became its own 'site of struggle with a new group of protagonists, mainly professors who held competing views of how to build Black studies'.[15] As Black studies distanced itself from its activist roots, it became clear that institutionalisation and professionalisation would turn overt activism into quiet revolt. Black studies, it seemed, had failed to realise its radical potential.[16]

Afro-pessimism (often called AP 2.0 to distinguish it from an unrelated discourse with the same name) emerged out of the very University of California system that had been a hotbed of Black studies radicalism in the 1960s. Its main proponents, Frank B. Wilderson III and fellow UC professor Jared Sexton, founded the philosophical movement following a two-day symposium titled 'Black Thought in the Age of Terror' at UC Irvine in 2006.[17] Wilderson and Sexton were responding to a general feeling of despair that had gripped Black America. While the sense was, again, that little had changed for Black people since the Civil Rights era – gratuitous violence against Black people by the US State or discrimination by legal, educational, cultural, scientific or medical institutions are still commonplace today – AP 2.0 responded by calling for retreat instead of revolt. In the late nineties, Wilderson had been a radical student activist involved with the Third World Liberation Front (he once led a courtroom occupation which resulted in the release of six members of the group who were on trial).[18] But by the mid-2000s, such radicalism had given way to a more meditative approach which fused his insights from years of activism with philosophical reflections on the state of Black people in the world today.[19] Wilderson and Sexton's endeavour was provocative and wildly successful. As Greg Tate put it, 'Black intellectuals [hadn't] enjoyed this much pop currency among the right wing since Black Power took over buildings to demand Black studies in state universities and the Ivies 50 years ago'.[20]

AP 2.0 has inspired equally impassioned responses on the left.[21] This is largely because of its divisive central premise. Drawing on the sociologist Orlando Patterson's writings, Wilderson – the most controversial figure associated with the movement – argues that the condition of Black people is not characterised by oppression or exploitation, like that of the Marxist proletariat or the (neo-) colonial subject, but by the distinction between the 'Human' and the 'Slave'. In *Slavery and Social Death* (1982), Patterson uses the concept of social death to point to the condition of enslaved Black people prior to abolition. Enslaved people owned no property and had no legal claims to family or land, and could therefore not be considered modern subjects. Sexton, too, has argued that the social reality of the Black/Slave is one of total powerlessness, natal alienation ('the loss of ties of birth in both ascending and descending generations') and generalised dishonour.[22] While Patterson, who has distanced himself from AP 2.0's pessimism, uses social death as a historical concept, Wilderson asserts that Black existence (or rather non-existence) is characterised by the condition of 'the Slave'. According to Wilderson, we cannot speak of Blackness without reference to the 'slaveness' that constitutes it on an ontological level.[23]

AP 2.0 insists that Blackness is a sort of ontological absence, which turns the Black/Slave – as Black people are often referred to in AP 2.0 theories – into a living dead (non-entity) in the modern world. This tendency to place Black people outside of the realm of humanity (and therefore *being*) is perhaps best exemplified by Calvin Warren who, in his 2018 book *Ontological Terror*, painstakingly strikes through the word 'being' every time it is used in relation to Blackness. Because the condition of the Black/Slave is characterised by social death, their struggles are qualitatively different from those of other oppressed peoples. 'The point of social death', writes Wilderson in 'The Black Liberation Army and the Paradox of Political Engagement', 'is a condition, void, not of land, but of a capacity to secure relational status through transindividual objects – be those objects elaborated by land, labor, or love.'[24] Unlike colonial racisms perpetuated by the rational systems of white supremacy, neocolonialism or imperialism, or women's oppression and exploitation driven by patriarchy and capitalism's need for reproductive labour, anti-Black violence is humanity's irrational desire for violence against Black people. As Wilderson puts it in a 2015 interview, 'Violence against Black people is a mechanism for the usurpation of subjectivity, of life, of being'.[25] AP 2.0 claims that the modern world relies on anti-Black violence to reproduce itself. So, 'as long as the world exists, this murder must continue'.[26]

The most concerning aspect of AP 2.0, however, is that it precludes the possibility of the kind of anti-imperialist solidarity championed by Bandung-era movements like the Non-Aligned Movement, the Tricontinental or the Third World Liberation Front. Because anti-Blackness is qualitatively different from the regimes of violence that affect the Marxist proletariat, or the non-Black person of colour, or the non-Black woman, or the non-Black woman of colour, or (as Wilderson has infamously claimed) Palestinians, we cannot speak of any experience of oppression without reference to the ontological disparities between Black/non-Black people.[27] To not speak of these disparities, he argues, would be an act of anti-Blackness. For Wilderson, there can be no solidarity between Black people and the oppressor (white men) or their 'junior partners' (all non-Black people).[28] The claim that Black people and Palestinians cannot form bonds of solidarity is derived from a conversation with a Palestinian co-worker, Sameer Bishara, whom Wilderson befriended while working at the Walker Art Center in Minneapolis. Remembering how he was harassed at Israeli checkpoints, Sameer makes the offhand comment that the humiliation was made worse by the fact that the policemen were Ethiopian Jews. Wilderson takes this to mean that Sameer, and by extension all Palestinians, shared their Israeli oppressors 'negrophobogenesis' (negrophobia). In his memoir, the ensuing theorisation of Sameer's anti-Blackness takes place mainly as an internal monologue; we don't hear any more from Sameer, who is never given the chance to explain his comment. Wilderson, it seems, already has all the answers.

This is a view of the world that is, true to its name, entirely pessimistic. For AP 2.0 there can be no political resistance, because the very foundations of political discourse are inherently anti-Black. Or, to put it in terms of political ontology, 'the political' – the ontological character of a political situation that separates it from other social actions – is skewed against the Black/Slave.[29] Participation in the political sphere is based on the recognition of the other's humanity, which then enables this other to challenge the order on its own grounds. But since the Black is a priori a Slave, and Blackness and slaveness are coterminous, the Black/Slave cannot participate in the Symbolic Order as their status is not that of the Human. And because the category of humanity is founded and relies on the existence of the slave, there is no way the Black/Slave can ever gain the recognition required to assert political demands and identities in the political sphere. It is for this reason, Sexton argues, that we must posit a 'political ontology dividing the Slave from the world of the Human in a constitutive way' and take this as our analytical starting point.[30] When it comes to the question of political strategy, AP 2.0 defers to activists on the ground. Wilderson makes this clear when he states that that he can offer only an analysis of the problem, not a solution.[31]

AP 2.0 might seem like a niche theoretical discourse, but its anti-politics of despair resonate outside of the halls and lecture theatres of universities. As Annie

Olaloku-Teriba has argued, AP 2.0's theoretical framework provides the 'structuring logic of various political formations in the era of #BlackLivesMatter'.[32] The term 'anti-Blackness', for example, which is central to AP 2.0's theoretical vocabulary, has become common parlance in activist spaces. But what can explain AP 2.0's staying power despite its obvious theoretical flaws? Adolph Reed Jr. rightly suspects that the popular appeal of theories of despair might have something to do with Black people losing faith in the ideal of a 'post-racial' United States.[33] Small improvements in individual upward mobility in the last fifty years did little to address racial inequalities. Moreover, the ongoing cycle of state violence against Black people in the US seems to be never-ending. When a nationwide rebellion broke out following the murder of George Floyd by police in the spring of 2020, AP 2.0's pessimism seemed to have been overtaken by actual political events. Here were millions of people across the world rising up in solidarity with Black people in the United States (and connecting their struggles to histories of police violence in countries like Nigeria and South Africa). Impossible, according to AP 2.0. But as the rebellion faded, things quickly returned to 'normal'.[34] The appeal of the idea that nothing 'is going to stop these cops from killing us' arises from such disappointments.[35] Yet wouldn't it be more productive to ask why the rebellion couldn't achieve its aims? Could it have something to do with the absence of an organisation that is able transform its demands into lasting change?

AP 2.0 contributes to a wider debate on the nature of Black studies in the United States. The scholars engaged in this debate all share a common interest in the 'afterlife of slavery' first described by Saidiya Hartman in her 2006 memoir *Lose Your Mother*. Though Reed treats AP 2.0 and Hartman's writing as part of the same tradition of 'race reductionism', there are significant differences between their accounts of the afterlife of slavery. For Hartman, the official abolition of slavery in the United States did not engender a decisive break with the racialised violence of slavery. We can see traces of this violence today in the 'skewed life chances, limited access to health and education, premature death, incarceration, and impoverishment' of Black people.[36] Formal abolition and Reconstruction did not lead to emancipation. Instead, these events served as points of 'transition between modes of servitude and racial subjection'.[37] By foregrounding the violent process of racial subjection, Hartman wants to show that the violence of slavery is not limited to the 'construction of the slave as object'; in fact, enslaved people's humanity was central to the project of racial subjection.[38] Black people, then, are not subhuman objects, as Wilderson, Sexton and Warren claim, but racialised subjects who are very much part of the social and political sphere.

Unlike AP 2.0, Hartman emphasises Black people's ability to resist. In *Wayward Lives, Beautiful Experiments* (2019), she employs the method of 'critical fabulation' to uncover the stories of young Black women and gender non-conforming people in the United States at the turn of the twentieth century. In cities like New York and Philadelphia, these women, only a few generations out of slavery, were subjected to new forms of racialised and gendered servitude or oppression. Hartman argues that these Black women were engaging in 'minor' revolutions to 'create autonomous and beautiful lives, to escape the new forms of servitude awaiting them, and to live as if they were free'. Hartman crafts a counter-narrative to the official archive, where we tend to encounter either silence or erasure when looking for evidence of these wayward lives. In a brief theoretical note, she reminds us that the term 'wayward' is related to the family of words that includes 'errant, fugitive, recalcitrant, anarchic, wilful, reckless, troublesome, riotous, tumultuous, rebellious and wild'.[39] Her project builds on the American anarchist tradition ('though she had not read *God and the State* or *What Is Property?* or *The Conquest of Bread*, the dangers she and others like her posed was as great as . . . Emma Goldman and Alexander Berkman'), but is never limited by it.[40] Rather, it is a Black radical practice that cannot be reduced to other political ideologies.

AP 2.0 has claimed many a Black thinker as its supposed ally. But their own work doesn't always sit comfortably alongside the Black scholars whose work they, to borrow a phrase from Gloria Wekker, 'cannibal-ise'.[41] Hortense Spillers, for example, whom AP 2.0 often claims as one of their own, has complained about the discourse's reification of Blackness, which ignores its inherent dynamism. For Spillers, AP 2.0 is a deeply conservative project that takes Blackness, which is usually a point of departure for our analysis, as a point of arrival. AP 2.0's conservatism extends to its treatment of Black feminist thought, too. (Wekker suggests that Black studies departments in US universities today are still dominated by Black men, making Black middle-class masculinity the 'unspoken, unquestioned starting point' of many of the field's analyses.) Wilderson's perspective is marked by the erasure of feminist thought from his theorisation of Black social death; for him, patriarchy, for example, does not constitute a form of oppression. And while he sometimes pays lip service to Black feminism, he 'always places the category of "race" above other simultaneous grammars of difference such as gender, class and sexuality'.[42] AP 2.0's project, then, is not the same as that of Hartman, whose queer and feminist politics are visible throughout her writing.

AP 2.0 finds a more comfortable interlocutor in Fred Moten, whose theory of Black optimism pushes back against the concept of social death by foregrounding Black agency. For Moten, Black agency is prior to the all-encompassing anti-Blackness of the modern world. Drawing on traditions of *marronage* – Black runaway slaves who escaped the plantations and formed settlements in the hills and swamps of Jamaica or Florida – Moten casts 'fugitivity' as a mode of Black resistance. His work draws heavily from the writing of the anarchist anthropologist James C. Scott, whose work focuses on the ability of various peoples to live without states, and avoid being incorporated into states, in South and Southeast Asia as well as Southern China. As Moten and his frequent collaborator Stefano Harney note, these people were often 'known in the language of those who hunted them, those who lived in states, by the word in those state languages for "slave", even before they became enslaved'.[43] This is a form of Black resistance that is resolutely non-statist and casts refusal as the only revolutionary strategy. The organic relationship between anti-statism and Black resistance is perhaps best illustrated by the maroons who developed systems of small-scale agriculture, which allowed for self-sufficient food production, after the reinstatement of the plantocracy in the wake of the Haitian revolution (see chapter 3). According to Moten and Harney, those who theorise Black life as social death have failed to understand that fugitivity ('an ensemble of living practices') was central to enslaved people's existence.[44]

Moten and Harney draw parallels between the resistance of the formerly enslaved maroons and Black (or marginalised) academics working in what they call 'the undercommons', a space outside of official political and institutional structures, where they can assert their 'right to refuse'. The undercommons refers to those who have been written off by the university as unprofessional and lack the job security, living wages, health benefits or professionalised resources of their better-off colleagues.[45] The privatisation and professionalization of the university discussed above has made it increasingly difficult for academics to become activist-intellectuals. Trapped in a cycle of precarious employment, low pay, pressure to publish, excessive teaching and marking duties and so on, the inhabitants of the undercommons cannot meet the excessive demands of the neoliberal university. Therefore, they refuse to accommodate, or be incorporated by, the institution. The hope that their frustration with the working conditions in the university might spark a revolt is Moten and Harney's response to the institutionalisation and deradicalisation of Black studies. But this is not the organised and planned resistance of political revolution. Their theory builds on Cedric Robinson's critique of the 'terms of order' of Western civilisation, which, he argues, is a project that is rooted in a desire to unsettle the political, understood as both an 'instrument for ordering society and that order itself'.[46] For Robinson, as for Moten and Harney, resistance to the political arises not from Marxian conceptions of proletarian struggle, but from an improvised politics of Black anarchism.

Moten's Black optimism, however, fails to break with some of AP 2.0's theoretical premises. In a long essay on the anti-colonial thinker Frantz Fanon, he writes that 'Black optimism and Afro-pessimism are asymptotic', and that their disagreement, or 'non-meeting', is part of a 'minor internal conflict'.[47] The association of Black optimism and AP 2.0, then, is closer than it might seem. As Olaloku-Teriba points out in her excellent critique of the AP 2.0, it finds a 'comfortable antagonist' in Moten, whose Black optimism can be neatly reintegrated into the concept of social death.[48] It is telling that Sexton rather successfully merges the two, arguing that 'a living death is as much a death as it is living'. According to Sexton, AP 2.0 doesn't claim that there is no Black social life, but rather that Black life 'is not social life in the universe formed by the codes of state and civil society, of citizen and subject, of nation and culture, of people and place, of history and heritage' and all other markers of the modern world system.[49] Moten, too, acknowledges that he is sympathetic to the claim that Black people are excluded from the political sphere. For Moten, the expulsion of Black life from the political and its relegation to the field of the social constitutes the Black subject's social death. Technically speaking, then, it is not a social but a political death. Yet Moten's theory, like AP 2.0, precludes Black people's participation in radical politics by confining resistance to spaces outside of the political sphere.[50]

AP 2.0 frequently erases or distorts beyond recognition the various Black liberation movements that fought against racism, colonialism and imperialism throughout the global south – especially the African national liberation struggles. In 'The Avant-Garde of White Supremacy', Steve Martinot and Sexton claim that anti-colonial thought treats racism as a 'social ideology that can be refuted, a structure of privilege to be given up, again at the local or individual level'.[51] Anti-colonial discourses, they argue, 'subsume the issue of racism in promises of future transformations of power relations to which racialisation is deferred' and assume that it will disappear if it is 'no longer useful to the relations of production or the security of territorial boundaries'. Wilderson makes a similar claim, arguing that anti-colonial movements' misdiagnosis of racism stems from their fundamentally different positionality in relation to anti-Blackness: while the 'postcolonial' can quite literally throw the settler out of their zone, the Black/Slave must throw the Human out of their zone if they are to overcome the condition of social death that characterises Black life.[52] ('Postcolonial' and 'anti-colonial' are often used interchangeably by Wilderson, Sexton and Martinot.) The postcolonial subject exists as Human in the symbolic order, whereas the Black/Slave can never; this, Wilderson insists, is what the Black/Slave Fanon of *Black Skin, White Masks* (1952) understood, but the postcolonial Fanon of *The Wretched of the Earth* (1967) did not.[53] This misreading of Fanon, and anti-colonial politics more broadly, is addressed in chapters 5 to 7.

When reading over AP 2.0 bibliographies, one can be forgiven for thinking that the sheer number of references to radical scholarship reflects a close reading and consideration of the texts in question. This is not the case. Martinot and Sexton, for example, claim that Marxism treats racism as merely a divide-and-conquer strategy employed by the bourgeoisie to maintain class rule and prevent workers from realising their shared interests.[54] Marxism, they argue, has failed to understand that racism – and anti-Black racism in particular – is not an ideology that can be refuted; instead, it is 'fundamental to class relations themselves'. Wilderson offers a similar critique, arguing that the Black/Slave poses an insoluble problem for the Gramscian discourse on race, since anti-Black racism is driven by the 'despotism of the unwaged relation' and not the exploitation of wage labour. For Wilderson, Marxism has failed to think anything other than capitalism as the 'base' structure from which other superstructural phenomena such as racism emerge. Marxists have thus failed to recognise that 'capital was kick-started by the rape of the African continent', which is 'as close to capital's primal desire than is waged oppression'. The mere existence of the Black/Slave troubles the foundational premises of Marxist thought, thereby rendering Marxism's theoretical tools useless for the analysis of the afterlife of slavery. This is the supposed 'scandal of historical materialism'.[55] But, as we will see in the following chapter, this account of Marxism isn't quite accurate.

The final aspect of AP 2.0 which warrants further analysis is its account of slavery. Wilderson thinks that slavery is 'relational' and not 'historical', which might help explain why his grasp of global histories of slavery is so limited.[56] The theorisation of the Black/Slave relies almost entirely on the experiences of US chattel slavery, though it only accounted for about 4 per cent of all enslaved Africans (ca. 12.5 million) that were transported to the Americas between the sixteenth and nineteenth century.

What about, one is tempted to ask, the Caribbean and Portuguese America, which were so crucial to the trans-atlantic slave trade? Close to five million enslaved Africans were taken to Portuguese America (now Brazil) between 1501 and 1866; their labour became the driving force for the sugar economy in the early seventeenth century and gold and diamond mining from about 1690 onwards.[57] Slavery was not abolished in Cuba until 1886 and in Brazil until 1888, yet AP 2.0 continues to structure its analysis of the afterlife of slavery around the abolition of slavery in the United States in 1865. If we want to understand how slavery shaped the politics of social formations across the world, we will have to move beyond such parochialism.

The 'anti-political' tendency in Black studies is most obvious in the theories of AP 2.0, but also present in the writing of Moten, Harney and Hartman. This retreat from organised politics is the result of the defeat of activist Black studies. It responds to this defeat, and the professionalization and institutionalisation of Black studies, either by withdrawing into despair (AP 2.0) or finding refuge in a form of Black anarchism that is hostile to Marxian notions of political revolution (Moten, Harney and Hartman).[58] This anti-political tendency shares four key features. First, a theoretical critique of Marxism which claims that it is either Eurocentric, unable (or unwilling) to conceptualise Black struggle, or unable to account for the forms of domination that characterised slavery.[59] Second, its analysis of Blackness remains closely tied to a history of racial politics that is specific to the United States. Third, it elevates the perspective of diaspora scholars in the global north over those of struggles in the global south. And finally, it distrusts the supposedly state-centric politics of national liberation.[60] This critique of Marxism and national liberation works to erase a tradition of anti-colonial Marxism I call Red Africa.

3

Racial Capitalism and the Afterlives of Slavery

The claim that Marxism is Eurocentric isn't new. Cedric J. Robinson's *Black Marxism* (1983), for example, has become a key text for Black scholars and activists hoping to find proof of Marxism's Eurocentrism, or its inability to come to terms with questions of race and racism. While Robinson authored five monographs and numerous academic articles, he is best known for popularising the concept of racial capitalism. But, as Robin D.G. Kelley points out, Robinson's book 'was primarily about Black revolt, not racial capitalism' – racial capitalism was simply the context from which the spirit of Black revolt emerged.[1] But how did this idea of Black revolt differ from the Marxian promise of proletarian revolution? For Robinson, capitalism had a non-objective character: instead of universalising the wage relation, it had created racial and colonial categories to enshrine hierarchies such as the differentiation of waged and unwaged (surplus) labour. Because capitalism had failed to universalise the wage relation, it had also failed to create the universal class – the revolutionary industrial proletariat – which would bring about its demise. Robinson believed that racial capitalism didn't give rise to rational and organised opposition; instead, it engendered disorderly resistance which stood outside capitalism's terms of order and was thus better positioned to challenge its hegemony. What he called the Black radical tradition contained the seeds of racial capitalism's destruction – this was what Marx and Engels had not understood.

Robinson claimed that historical materialism relied on a theory of history based on a linear conception of time. As such, it promised that history would end once the class struggle – which had hitherto been the record of history – resulted in the eradication of classes in a future socialist society. But for much of human history, the 'linear construction of history would have been taken as an aberration'.[2] For Amílcar Cabral, as for Robinson, history didn't begin with the advent of classes and end once these had disappeared. There had been examples of classless societies before the advent of colonialism; subscribing to the Marxist view of history implied that these societies had lived outside history until they were 'subjected to the yoke of imperialism'.[3] And even after the class struggle, history would continue. (As Cabral put it, 'Eternity is not of this world, but man will outlive classes and will continue producing and making history'.[4]) In place of historical materialism, Robinson proposed an open dialectic, one which eschewed linear time in favour of a different, improvisatory temporality and truly captured the essence of Black revolt. Like Moten's undercommons, this is a form of resistance that is immanent to itself; in other words, Black radicalism always-already *is*. And while he never really liked the word 'utopian' – Avery F. Gordon writes that he felt it had a 'connotation of naiveté and impossibility' – there is a sense of precisely such utopianism in his idea of a spontaneously erupting Black radical tradition.[5]

Robinson's work helpfully points to the tension in Marxism between a teleological march towards progress – with revolution as the outcome of the contradiction between productive forces and the relations of production – and the spontaneous and mass-led character of revolution. But Robinson at times ignores the second, constructivist tendency in Marx, attributing to him only a rigid determinism. The evolutionary schema of social formations – from feudalism to capitalism, socialism and eventually communism – is not all there is to Marx's thought. We know, for example, that later in life Marx revised his position on the role of the peasantry and rural communes in the transition to socialism. In letters to his Russian critic Vera Zasulich, Marx conceded that it wasn't necessary to pass through the capitalist stage in Russia's transition to socialism. In later writings on non-Western and pre-capitalist societies, he took note of the revolutionary potential of class formations other than the Western industrial proletariat. It might be tempting to brush aside Marxism and its conception of time as 'teleological'. But, as Enzo Traverso has argued, there is a third dimension of time in Marx's writing, beyond the Hegelian view of history or the abstract time of capital: the disruptive time of revolution, a 'self-regulated time of human emancipation and agency'.[6] Considering that such texts were available to Robinson, it is surprising to not find this Marx, whose view of revolutionary time closely resembles his own, feature more prominently in *Black Marxism*.

But why had Marx, Engels and their followers failed to take note of the revolutionary potential of this Black radical tradition and its expression of working-class consciousness? For Robinson, there exists a direct lineage in Western thought, running from Plato and Aristotle to Marx and Engels, which disregards the significance of slavery in the making of Western civilisation. The classics of Western philosophy were composed by an intellectual class supported by unfree labour, and effectively worked to preserve the social structures which gave this class a privileged status in Greek society. Aristotle and Plato's treatment of slave labour, Robinson argues, anticipates the later disregard for other forms of unfree or non-industrial labour – indentured workers, peasants or women's unpaid labour – in Marxism.[7] Because Marxism's philosophical origins were indisputably Western, and its founders, Marx and Engels, themselves organic intellectuals not of the working class but of the European middle class, it had failed to truly break with bourgeois epistemology and its systems of differentiation. This was precisely why Marxism had been unable (or unwilling) to acknowledge racialism, one of the founding hierarchies of Western civilisation and, by extension, of capitalism. Marxism, then, was an insufficiently radical self-examination of Western civilisation; it could never be the radical alternative to political economy that it promised to be.

That Marx disregarded unfree or non-industrial labour in his writing is not entirely true. In volume 1 of *Capital*, for example, Marx clearly recognises that

the discovery of gold and silver in America, the extirpation, enslavement and entombment in mines of the indigenous population of that continent, the beginnings of the conquest and plunder of India, and the conversion of Africa into a preserve for the commercial hunting of blackskins, are all things which characterise the dawn of the era of capitalist production. These idyllic proceedings are the chief moments of primitive accumulation.[8]

In a letter to the Russian literary critic Pavel Vasilyevich Annenkov, Marx further explains that there is a fundamental difference between 'indirect slavery' (i.e., the wage slavery of the proletariat) and the condition of enslaved Black people 'in Surinam [sic], in Brazil, in the southern regions of North America'.[9] He makes a clear distinction between slave labour and wage labour, refusing to conflate both in the category of the proletariat. For Marx, the very possibility of a unified proletarian revolution relied on the abolition of slavery. But while it might at times sound like Marx is theorising race as a divide and conquer strategy – as many critics have accused him of doing – this doesn't necessarily mean that Marxism as a method incorporates this flawed analysis. There exists a tradition of Marxist thought which has taken seriously the role that the racial played in structuring the modern world, and which acknowledges how central both the transatlantic slave trade and racism were to the development of capitalism. We will see below how this tradition complicates the separation between the exploitation of the worker and the social death of the Black/Slave that is at the heart of AP 2.0's account of Blackness.

There is some confusion over what we mean by racial capitalism, with dismissive critics questioning the theoretical and political value of the concept.[10] Therefore, it is worth briefly tracing the history of the term to determine what racial capitalism really *is*. The 'promise of the term', says Arun Kundnani, 'lies in its apparent bridging of the economic and the cultural, of the class struggle and the struggle against white supremacy, allowing us to understand police and plantation violence as linked to capitalist accumulation'.[11] Though Robinson is frequently associated with the theory of racial capitalism, he didn't coin the term; its first use dates to a 1976 pamphlet titled *Foreign Investment and the Reproduction of Racial Capitalism in South Africa* written by the South African Marxists Martin Legassick and David Hemson.[12] In the late 1970s, the official position of the International Labour Organisation (ILO) was that a conflict existed between the objective of economic growth and the policy of apartheid, and that the former would eventually undermine and abolish the latter. According to the ILO, there was no need for mass anti-racist struggle – capital itself would do the necessary work. But Legassick and Hemson disagreed. Instead, they showed that racism in South Africa had intensified the more advanced the country's capitalist economy had become. Apartheid racism, then, was not some pre-modern prejudice that was alien to capitalism; it was a key part of the logic of capital accumulation in the country.

For Robinson, however, the South African case was not an exception but the rule; all capitalism, he argued, was racial. In emphasising the combined and uneven character of development – or, put differently, the coexistence of archaic and contemporary social, cultural and economic forms in a social formation – he wanted to show that capitalism tended to preserve older hierarchies instead of eradicating them. Racism was how it coded and preserved differentiation: 'As a material force, then, it could be expected that racialism would inevitably permeate the social structures emergent from capitalism.'[13] The value of Robinson's work lies in its ability to uncover the historically contingent relationship between Blackness and slavery. In *Black Marxism*, white supremacy masks itself as an economic rationale, which in turn organises racial hierarchy, with racialised plantation labour at its core. Beginning in early medieval period, a set of hierarchies which enabled domination based on racial characteristics had developed in Europe. When capitalism started to emerge several centuries later, these forms of racialism were mapped onto nascent class formations: the bourgeoisie, the peasantry and the enslaved each corresponded to certain ethnic and cultural groups. Racialism became the ordering principle used to justify the domination, exploitation or extermination of non-white (or 'non-European') peoples, whether Jewish, Irish or Slavic. Minor differences in dialect, region or culture were encoded as racial difference, as capitalism and racism grew together from the old feudal order to produce 'racial capitalism' – a world system that relies on slavery, violence, imperialism and genocide for its continued expansion.

When English merchant capital expanded into the Americas in the seventeenth century, African labour was incorporated into Europe's racial order. The form of racism which emerged in the Americas

did not replace nor displace its European antecedents . . . Rather it embellished the inventory of Western racism, extending its shape, and resubstantiating its force and authority by providing simultaneously a cruder and more defensible access to whichever forms the occasion demanded. This new racism, initially coincident with a slave social order, by the end of the nineteenth century was being adapted to the two most urgent impulses of industrial capital: the uncertain amalgamation of a white working class and the more enduring fabrication of an imperial national identity. It was in place as a social discipline when European immigrant labor flooded the factory gates of industrial America; and it was there as an historical justification when American imperialists smashed the Spanish Empire in the Philippines and the Caribbean.[14]

Early forms of racialism had allowed medieval European societies to legitimise hierarchical relationships as natural, in the same way race had allowed planters in the Americas to justify the use of indentured and later slave labour. There was, of course, a qualitative difference between the two. But one could trace a direct lineage from early European racialism and racism as it appeared today. Capitalism, Robinson demonstrated, was not a negation of feudalist society but an 'extension of these social relations into the larger tapestry of the modern world's political and economic relations'. Racism was not rooted in one specific era, and neither was it produced by one historical event; it was at the very heart of Western civilisation. Or, as Chris Chen similarly writes, the 'colonial and racial genealogy of European capitalism' was 'encoded directly into the economic "base" through an ongoing history of racial violence which . . . binds surplus populations to capitalist markets'.[15]

*　　*　　*

Instead of going back to what Marx did or didn't say about slavery, it might be more constructive to explore how the history of the transatlantic slave trade forces us to rethink the fundamental categories of the Marxist critique of political economy. We should follow Stephanie Smallwood in asking not what Marx tells us about slavery but what slavery tells us about Marx. Smallwood insists that 'Marx failed to adequately account for the origins of capitalism', though he did recognise that the slave trade played a key role in some way. Citing Marx's discussion of 'the working day' in *Capital*, Smallwood shows that Marx presented 'slave-trading in the Americas as *analogous* to the capitalist labor market in industrializing Europe that "produces the pre-mature exhaustion and death of labour power itself" '.[16] Far from consigning the slave trade to the prehistory of primitive accumulation, Marx here recognises that the use of enslaved labour constitutes a specifically capitalist form of exploitation (super-exploitation), where the wages a person receives for their work – in this case, none at all – are below the value of their labour power. Smallwood goes further by arguing that Marx's primitive accumulation is not only a starting point for capital accumulation but is *itself* a capitalist form of accumulation. But, she argues, Marx doesn't make this connection often enough, instead treating capitalism and New World slavery as analytically distinct. AP 2.0 has taken this separation as an unchangeable fact, claiming that it is impossible to address racial domination in relation to class exploitation within Marxism's theoretical frame.

There are two standard Marxist accounts of the relationship between early colonial capitalism and the European enslavement of Africans: the first treats slavery as part of the process of primitive accumulation (Robin Blackburn), while the second insists that enslaved labour is non-capitalist since capitalism is a system based on the exploitation of 'free' wage labour (Robert Brenner).[17] The Brenner school's argument is what AP 2.0 and other critics take to be the 'official' Marxist position, though it is hardly representative of Marxist thinking on enslavement and has been convincingly refuted by Nikhil Pal Singh, for example.[18] Robin Blackburn's historical studies of the transatlantic slave trade, however, offer a more nuanced Marxian perspective, which is entirely at odds with the straw man Marxism that many Black scholars and activists argue against.[19] Blackburn's work emphasises the interconnection between slavery, colonialism and capitalism; he, too, wants to understand how 'the racial' structures the mode of production (and exploitation) in each instance. Like early African, Islamic or Roman slavery, chattel slavery was based on the idea that a person could be bought and sold. But unlike prior forms of enslavement, US plantations institutionalised slavery, made it hereditary and intensified prior forms of racism.

Blackburn makes a distinction between the *ancillary* slavery of early Spanish and Portuguese colonialism and the *systemic* slavery of the eighteenth century to argue that enslaved plantation labour or indentured labour are not capitalist *proper* but part of a long history of primitive accumulation. While previous forms of slavery had been less commercial and institutionalised, systemic plantation slavery in the eighteenth century was based on a partnership between mercantile capital and planters, which established a tightly coordinated labour process that strongly resembled that of later industrial manufacturing. He rightly argues that the 'main motive for slaveholding [in the Americas] was economic exploitation', and that most enslaved labour was used to produce commodities.[20] Yet he also insists that we must distinguish 'between New World slavery and a regime of generalised commodity production' precisely because plantation slavery had its 'roots in the so-called "natural economy" – that is, subsistence cultivation and internal, "uncommodified" labour'.[21] But does this necessarily mean that the mode of exploitation at work on the plantations was not capitalist in nature? Could we not instead follow Walter Rodney in asking why capitalist exploitation should be restricted to surplus value extraction from free labour when it was 'the same capitalist' exploiting free, indentured and enslaved labour in various geographies to accrue his profits? Or could we not suggest, as Sidney Mintz does, that enslaved Africans transported to the Caribbean were 'thrust into a remarkably *industrial* setting for their time', and that this setting resembled a form of industrial manufacturing?[22] Perhaps this is what Smallwood means when she urges us to consider what slavery can teach us about Marx.

Andrew Higginbottom, too, argues that Marx did not develop a substantive analysis of plantation slavery and the mode of exploitation that drove capital accumulation in the Americas. But unlike Blackburn, he suggests that enslaved labour was not an extended primitive accumulation into the nineteenth century, but a form of capitalist super-exploitation.[23] Of course, Blackburn accepts that colonial plantation slavery is a mode of exploitation, albeit a more primitive one.[24] He also acknowledges the condition of the enslaved, and that they 'were given bare rations and expected to feed themselves by working for a day, or a day and a half, each week on the plots

given to them for that purpose'.[25] But he seems reluctant
to accept that the use of enslaved labour on the plantations was what we might call a racialised mode of exploitation that was parallel to manufacturing, the main
labour process in capitalist Europe at the time. As such,
slavery was not a pre-capitalist form, but represented
capitalism in its early stages as a mode of production.
While slavery was, indeed, qualitatively different to wage
labour – one need only consider the kind of racial oppression involved – it nonetheless contributed just as much to
the development of the capitalist mode of production.
Colonial slavery was thus an internal relation of capitalism, characterised by what Higginbottom calls 'racial
super-exploitation', the mode of exploitation dominant
in plantation societies and, as we will see in chapter 7,
some African colonial societies.[26]

The analysis of slavery cannot be separated from the
early stages of capitalist accumulation and the violent
expansion of European (early Spanish and Portuguese,
later British as well) colonialism in the Americas and
Caribbean, as well as later colonialism in Africa and Asia.
As Greg Thomas puts it, 'There is no system of slavery in
any part of the Americas that is not still settler colonial
slavery; no settler colonialism without chattel slavery or
racial slavery and their neo-slaveries'.[27] Walter Rodney
already recognised this when he showed that plantation
slavery in the Americas was indeed colonial slavery.
Plantation slavery, Rodney further notes, was 'perhaps
the most effective of the colonial forms of exploitation
that had been established'; the 'plantation was par excel-
lence a colonial form'.[28] At first, large-scale plantation
slavery was a private enterprise of groups of planters
acting in their own interests (i.e., without reference to the

objectives of the metropole). But their objectives began to align more closely, as planters received protection from the metropole and the metropole benefited from the profits that the plantations generated. Blackburn writes:

> Systemic slavery had to be colonial in character because the slave plantations needed naval and military guarantees to protect them from rivals and the threat of slave revolt. While ancillary slavery helped to reproduce empire, empire helped to reproduce systemic slavery.[29]

In some cases, the ideals of the planters and the metropole were in conflict. But the aspirations of the plantation colonies – patriotism, self-sufficiency, and a society 'free of the vices of the Old World' – relied on the continued existence of slavery. The alliance between planters and the imperial centre, which was at the very heart of the plantation society, remained intact.

Most Marxist accounts of slavery owe a huge debt to *Capitalism and Slavery*, written in 1944 by Eric Williams, the historian and future prime minister of Trinidad and Tobago. The book explores the interconnected roots of capitalism, racism, abolitionism and the transatlantic slave trade. Williams's book was arguably the first monograph to break with prevailing orthodoxy among historians by arguing that racism was a product of slavery, not its cause. Initially, he argued, a variety of peoples were employed as unfree labour in the Americas, from indentured European peasants to orphaned 'disreputable' women or Indigenous peoples. As Williams complained:

> Slavery in the Caribbean has been too narrowly identi-
> fied with the Negro. A racial twist has thereby been
> given to what is basically an economic phenomenon.
> Slavery was not born of racism: rather, racism was the
> unfree consequence of slavery. Unfree labour in the
> New World was brown, white, black, and yellow;
> Catholic, Protestant and pagan.[30]

The kind of labour planters employed often depended on
the specific crops they were growing and the economic
structure of the plantation society. In Cuba, for example,
tobacco was a free white industry cultivated on small
farms, while sugar was a Black slave industry mostly
cultivated on large plantations. But various circumstances
combined to 'promote the use of enslaved labour' – indentured white labourers could not offer the planters a stable
workforce, as they had to eventually be released, while
Africans were condemned to lifelong bondage – and
produce a 'new culture of racism . . . as slavery became
encoded with "race" and rationalised in this way'.[31] As
sugar plantations grew ever larger and replaced other
crops, there was a dire need for more workers; these were
supplied from West Africa through the transatlantic slave
trade. New world slavery solved the labour problem for
planters and facilitated the process of capitalist accumulation in Western Europe, with the use of racialised
enslaved labour at the centre of its economic and social
model.[32] Slavery in the Americas, then, was related to the
rise of capitalism as a world system, not the result of an a
priori anti-Blackness, as ontological accounts of race
would have us believe.

Williams insisted that profits from the slave trade
contributed significantly to capital accumulation in

Europe, which later enabled the Industrial Revolution and colonial expansion. He therefore concluded that slavery laid the foundations not only for eighteenth-century British capitalism, but for capitalism as a whole. However, as sugar plantations in the West Indies became less profitable, abolition became a sensible option for British traders and planters.[33] The disruption of trade between the American colonies and the British Caribbean contributed far more to the abolition of the transatlantic slave trade than the 1776 rebellion which resulted in the Declaration of Independence of the United States. The declining profitability of sugar meant that the British West Indies were no longer as important to British industrial capitalism as they once were. The British abolitionists who made a passionate case for abolition in Parliament were not actually the heroes they'd been made out to be. Their moral arguments hadn't single-handedly ended the slave trade; it was simply economically reasonable to do so, since free trade (based on unequal exchange) replaced slavery as the primary source of profits for industrial development in England.[34] And though Williams 'did allot some weight to slave resistance and to the idealism of the abolitionists', he insisted that the economic structure of British colonial and commercial policy – in this case, 'the demotion of British West Indies as a result of the surge of trade with India and Latin America' – was more important. In any case, slavery had become a redundant form of surplus value extraction for colonial capitalism, and no longer constituted a significant fraction of total imperial wealth.[35]

But Robinson showed that this was not the case: instead of abolishing slavery, capitalism had incorporated its logic – the plantocracy survived its predicted demise.[36]

Even after formal abolition, the coercion of labour continued under the guise of wage slavery, debt peonage, share
cropping and forced or penal labour. After the formal
abolition of slavery, many planters used other types of
unfree labour to fill the gaps on their plantations. This
showed that emancipation had not come about purely
because capitalism didn't need unfree labour anymore, it
just needed to reconfigure the *kind* of unfree labour it
could use. Moreover, between the late eighteenth and the
early twentieth century, Saint-Domingue and the British
West Indies were at the height of their prosperity and
commercial profitability.[37] As Blackburn explains:

> The revolutionary events of this epoch thus brought
> about a simultaneous and fundamental restructuring
> of slavery and empire. The broad picture is clear
> enough. In the United States and Brazil, the colonial
> relationship was successfully rejected but slavery
> survived – indeed flourished. In Haiti and mainland
> Spanish America both slavery and colonial rule were
> defeated. In the British and French West Indies slavery
> was suppressed but colonial rule survived. The only
> flourishing slave colony left in the Americas by 1850
> was Spanish Cuba: a new colonial pact had been nego-
> tiated, born of the slaveholders' fear of the slaves and
> the willingness of an impoverished metropolis to allow
> the development of a rich slave colony.[38]

The abolition of slavery in the Americas was profoundly
uneven, developing out of a complex dialectic of resistance involving European and American abolitionists –
who, Blackburn points out, were often bourgeois but not
necessarily capitalist – commercial interests, class struggle

and Black resistance. Williams was right to argue that there were economic considerations at play in the process of abolition – it was a minor financial setback for both the imperial centre and the planters, who were rarely expropriated and sometimes even benefited from financial compensation schemes after the introduction of anti-slavery legislation – but he failed to take seriously the political factors.

The events of the Haitian Revolution, the largest and most successful slave rebellion in modern history, and the most radical of the uprisings that make up the Age of Revolution (1770–1850), illustrate this well. Colonial Saint-Domingue was 'the world's largest producer of sugar and coffee, along with significant amounts of cotton, indigo and cacao'. Moreover, it was one of the strongest export economies in the Americas, with a system of production that of course relied entirely on the use of enslaved labour: 'By the late eighteenth century there were 500,000 slaves in the colony, a majority of whom were born in Africa and worked under gruelling conditions in the plantations'.[39] French Saint-Domingue was the most profitable, and deadly, sugar colony in the world: it was so profitable that 'the masters found it economical to work their field slaves to death'.[40] But with oppression and exploitation came resistance:

From the mid 1750s [slaves] began to develop various kinds of individual and collective resistance. They formed brotherhoods in the plantations and practised *vodou* spirituals involving dance, song, possessions and divination, while *marrons* escaped in increasing numbers, retreating to the bush where they formed bands, or hiding in plain sight in towns and cities and spread ideas about emancipation.[41]

This set the stage for the long revolutionary struggle (1791–1804) which saw the enslaved revolt against the plantation owners in a heroic act of self-emancipation that reverberated across the Atlantic and 'successfully defended the gains of the French Revolution against France itself'.[42] (Napoleon had tried but failed to re-enslave the liberated Black people of Haiti who had taken to heart the French revolution's demands for liberty and equality for all.) This episode – captured with poise and clarity in C.L.R. James's masterpiece, *The Black Jacobins* (1938) – set the stage for further uprisings in the Caribbean and across the Americas, marking a key moment in Black radical history. While there had been prior slave uprisings in Saint-Domingue, the Haitian revolution politicised slave resistance, transforming it from simple rebellion into a universal call for emancipation.

There is no shortage of excellent studies of the Haitian Revolution or the lives of the revolutionary 'Black Spartacus', Toussaint Louverture, and his general Jean-Jacques Dessalines (see 'Further Reading'); in any case, there is no need to rehash these here. But the period after the revolution might help us better understand why theorists such as Fred Moten and Stefano Harney make fugitivity their central category of Black resistance. Johnhenry Gonzalez has argued that the period after the revolution was defined not only by the formation of a nation-state or the legal abolition of slavery, but by the development of a system of small-scale agriculture which allowed for self-sufficient domestic food production.[43] The persistence of the plantation society in

Haiti beyond the official abolition of slavery meant that legal emancipation often did not protect formerly enslaved people from forced labour (post-revolutionary Haiti certainly was no abolitionist utopia). The newly freed workers reacted by escaping to settlements to engage in autonomous food production. These settlements would come to define the post-revolutionary Haitian social formation and shape the country's cultural and economic identity as it transitioned from a plantation colony to a small-scale farming society. This is the fugitive marronage that Moten champions in his work.

Gonzalez uses the 'lens of marronage to interpret the survival strategies of Haiti's poor masses', and to trace their counter-institutional practices. He argues that agricultural development in post-revolutionary Haiti was instituted not by the state but by maroons who resisted the push to return to the sugar plantations, which were struggling because of declining profits from plantation exports. Gonzalez's analysis of Black resistance is characteristic of historical and theoretical accounts of fugitivity, and narrows in on 'questions of flight, clandestinity, and the emergence of runaway communities'.[44] But Black resistance did not always take this form. In 'Plantation Society in Guyana' (1981), Rodney shows that the thesis that former slaves fled the plantation en masse does not hold up in the case of post-abolition Guyana. Many formerly enslaved Black people moved off the plantations to small villages, which did not necessarily mean that they stopped working on these very plantations. It was not a withdrawal of plantation labour, but a move that allowed them to gain freedom and political power.[45] Some formerly enslaved people became a rural proletariat – which existed alongside, or as part of, a 'reconstituted peasantry' – who engaged in struggles against plantations owners and capital.[46] In short, this was a direct confrontation with the capitalist system that was undoubtedly an instance of class struggle. *Marronage* was just one form of resistance, and maroons constituted only a fraction of the peasantry (or rural proletariat) which existed after abolition.

Though marronage was certainly important in the Haitian Revolution (and the struggles of the Haitian masses after), 'skilled or "elite" slaves often played a leading role in plantation revolts and urban conspiracies'.[47] Black resistance to slavery was marked by the diversity of subjectivities and class positions inhabited by Black people in colonial plantation society, but the pressures of slavery had created new forms of sociality which brought together Black enslaved people in their common antagonism to the ruling order. One such example is, of course, the creation of Caribbean *creole*, a hybrid mixture of colonial, African and Indigenous languages. Another is *vodou*, an Afro-Haitian religion, which played a leading role in the revolution, but was banned afterwards because of its insurrectionary potential. In his part-historical, part-fictional (and undeniably political) retelling of slave resistance in *Counternarratives* (2016), John Keene – who gives equal space to the specificities of slavery in Brazil under Portuguese rule and in the pre–Civil War United States – weaves together these diverging but interconnected histories to draw out the underlying logic structuring gender, race and class under different forms of slavery and colonisation.[48] Most importantly, however, Keene plays with the engrained Eurocentric prejudices that colonisers used to belittle and 'other' enslaved and colonial subjects. Irrationality and spirituality become sources of power: Keene's characters really possess the magical powers that have been attributed to them; these are in turn transformed into a means for Black insurgency.

The multiple histories of Black resistance are also the subject of Stella Dadzie's 2020 book *A Kick in the Belly*, which challenges widespread misconceptions about the passivity of enslaved Black women in the British Caribbean. 'The ever-present threat of repression', Dadzie writes, 'was no match for the dreams and resentment of "turbulent" women, whose responses ranged from small daily acts of non-cooperation to major acts of rebellion'.[49] Dadzie shows that enslaved Black women resisted not only by escaping the plantation or refusing to perform the reproductive labour that kept the plantations going, but also by directly confronting their masters. There is the story of Minelta, a fifteen-year-old girl who is sentenced to death for attempting to poison her master, and feels no remorse; or that of Baby, who succeeded in murdering her owner; or the story of Cubah, the 'Queen of Kingston', who played a key role in an insurrection of Creole and Coromantee enslaved people against the British imperial forces in St Mary's parish in Jamaica in 1760. As Dadzie notes, 'Women ran away less often than men did and were also more likely to be caught, especially when they fled with children'.[50] But this also meant that they had to find means of rebellion that went beyond absconding. For enslaved Black women, murder or political insurrection were as much a part of the repertoire of resistance as marronage; this is what theorists of (Black) fugitivity seem to forget.

In Nigeria, the country with the world's largest Black population, the 'afterlife of slavery' takes on a completely different meaning than in the US. While slavery had existed in Igbo society before colonisation, it accelerated with the increasing demand for slaves on the other side of the Atlantic. When slavery was officially abolished in many parts of the West, Adiele Eberechukwu Afigbo writes in *The Abolition of the Slave Trade in Southeastern Nigeria, 1885–1950*, Igbo slave markets were flooded with *ohu* and *osu* slaves, whose descendants to this day retain the stigma of their ancestors: they cannot intermarry with the free-born and are excluded from important community organisations.[51] Adaobi Tricia Nwaubani, whose great-grandfather was a Nigerian slave trader, similarly observes that 'Igbo discrimination is not based on race, and there are no visual markers to differentiate slave descendants from freeborn. Instead, it trades on cultural beliefs about lineage and spirituality'.[52]

Discrimination of slave descendants is thus based on their role as outsiders, since they never really lost the status of the enslaved in a society where community ties are extremely important. Afigbo's periodisation also points to another important aspect of slavery in Nigeria: it was only officially abolished by the British in the early twentieth century but continued informally for at least another forty to fifty years. What this means is that we cannot understand slavery in Nigeria within the Igbo system through a concept of race conditioned entirely by the experiences of US chattel slavery. For the descendants of enslaved people in Nigeria, the afterlife of slavery is not characterised by the condition of the Black/Slave, as Wilderson and Sexton suggest, but by something quite different. In this case, the equation of the Black/Slave with the African does not hold, as this is a form of slavery that does not fit neatly within the genealogy of North American racial categories.

The Indian Ocean slave trade provides another example of a form of slavery that AP 2.0 cannot account for. Islam initially made its way south of the Sahara via the Red Sea, Egypt, Cyrenaica, Ifriqiya and the Maghrib through 'pre-existing caravan routes which linked the commercial centres of Northern Africa with those of southern, eastern and western Africa'.[53] The Sahel region, Rahmane Idrissa reminds us, was once known as *Bilad as-Sudan*, 'the country of the Blacks':

> The Sahel, then, was the narrow band of arid steppe immediately south of the Sahara, where Arab caravans crossing 'the sea' of the desert from the north docked in 'ports' such as Timbuktu and Biru . . . Beyond it lay the *terra firma* of the western Sudan – savanna bisected by the great loop of the Niger River – and its riches: gold, and the people who could be enslaved because they were born outside the Dar al-Islam.[54]

By the tenth century, an association between Blackness and certain forms of slavery had developed in the Arab world; the Indian Ocean trade in African slaves had brought a racial element to Islamic slavery. Yet it differed in both kind and scale from the transatlantic slave trade. Alexis de Tocqueville already noticed this in the years of the July Monarchy (1830–48), when he wrote that slavery in the Islamic world presented itself in a 'milder' form than in the West, and that Tunisia, for example, was actively looking to abolish slavery, while it continued in the French colonies and the United States.[55] Moreover, as Alexandre Popović points out, Indian Ocean trade never transformed into colonial slavery – this was, at least partly, due to slave uprisings like the Zanj Rebellion.[56] In the ninth century, enslaved Africans were transported from East Africa to Basra (Lower Iraq) and given the laborious task of making the marshland suitable for agricultural development. But the enslaved soon began to resist.[57] Led by Ali ibn Muhammad – an Arab Islamic scholar of mysterious origin – they banded together to challenge the Abbasid Caliphate and demand freedom. Popović notes that the rebellion was by no means a social revolution aimed at abolishing slavery; instead, it was a fifteen-year uprising in which enslaved Africans freed themselves and attempted to enslave their masters. The rebellion was eventually crushed by the caliphate's forces. But it had lasting effects and discouraged the use of racialised slavery for agricultural production in the region.

There are both 'continuities and changes between colonial plantation slavery in the Caribbean and Latin America, for example, and later nineteenth century chattel slavery' on cotton plantations in the Southern United States.[58] Yet these differences should not be glossed over too quickly. The racial hierarchies that structured plantation societies in Spanish, Portuguese and French colonies differed markedly from the binary racial categories – either Black or white – that governed colonies in North America, which had a comparatively large white settler population. Other colonies tolerated free Black and mixed-race people, who could themselves own enslaved people. In Spanish and Portuguese America enough formerly enslaved people, or their offspring, had obtained manumission to create a sizeable free Black and multiracial population. But 'only in the English colonies was there so small a free black population that nearly every black was a slave'.[59] Brazilian plantation society was based on hierarchical structures in which 'dress, manners and money "lightened" skin' – in this context, it would have made less sense to maintain a US-style racial order to uphold the institution of slavery.[60] Yet it is, of course, true that the type of slavery instituted in the British colonies, especially in the US, in the eighteenth century 'most consummately expressed the de-humanization of those who were now mere instruments of labour and chattels, subject to regular sale on the market'.[61]

So, what can we learn from these different histories of slavery and racialisation? The Brazilian scholar Denise Ferreira da Silva draws the following conclusion in her comparative study of race in the US and Brazil:

> I was convinced that our shared blackness has been traversed by the particular effects of specific nation, gender and class conditions. Slavery and colonialism composed the historical ground upon which race, gender and nationness have written the various versions of black subjectivity ... That intrinsically multiple quality of black subjectivity demands attention to the specific historical and discursive developments informing a society's strategies of racial subordination.[62]

In her 2007 book *Toward a Global Idea of Race*, Ferreira da Silva further contends that we cannot comprehend the 'present global configuration' unless we 'unpack how the racial, the cultural and the nation institute the modern subject' and analyse the context in which the modern subject emerged and was produced.[63] Racial difference, then, is responsible for structuring the contemporary world. And precisely because race supplies the discursive basis for the subordination of non-white people, specific studies of Blackness must be placed within the global historical context in which racialised subjects emerged. In this way, we can avoid parochial ontological conceptions of Blackness while simultaneously emphasising the histories of interconnection between Black people across the world. In short, the object of analysis is not only the afterlife of slavery in the United States, but the multiplicity of afterlives of both slavery and colonisation; the aim is to study how these exist within a global system structured by imperialism.

4
Négritude and the (Mal)practice of Diaspora

In the 1930s, a group of young émigrés from different parts of the French colonial empire set out to develop an aesthetic framework designed to counter historical and cultural narratives that exclusively ascribed the properties of beauty and goodness to anything white and European. In Paris, the metropolitan centre of the French colonial empire, these intellectuals found themselves united by a common experience: as educated and sophisticated *évolués* – French colonial subjects who had 'evolved' by assimilating European values and gaining a European education – they had not expected to face racial prejudice. For the French, however, they were still colonial subjects that belonged to a race of people considered uncivilised and in need of guidance. A privileged class position within the colonies could not shield them from their visible 'otherness' in the metropole, and for the first time they became aware of what 'Africanness' and 'Blackness' really meant for the French.

In its initial iteration, Négritude was an artistic expression that sought to re-appropriate the term *art nègre* and strip it of its racist connotations. These intellectuals and artists wanted to deconstruct Western society from within, turning its own language and concepts – French and Surrealism – against it, with the aim of showing that its supposedly enlightened values were the same ones that were used to justify slavery and colonialism. As part of a group of non-white Surrealists that included Aimé and Suzanne Césaire, Étienne Léro, Yva Léro, Wifredo Lam, and René Menil, the Négritude poets asserted the value of a distinctly Black identity, which was entirely at odds with the French colonial policy of assimilationism.[1] Their aim was to capture the beauty and vitality of African bodies, culture and history, and to throw them back in the faces of the French. Western rationality was juxtaposed with African emotion, and the Bergsonian *élan vital* of the African held up as the creative force driving Black cultural production.

While the Négritude poets all had different interpretations of what the term really meant, the most common characterisation of the movement comes from the French philosopher Jean-Paul Sartre who, in 'Black Orpheus' (1948), argued that Négritude was an 'anti-racist racism'.[2] For Sartre, Négritude was an important negation of whiteness – but the assertion of this essentialist Blackness was a negative moment in the dialectic, which would soon be overtaken by a universal consciousness embodied in the struggle of the proletariat for communism. Sartre's essays have too often shaped how twentieth-century African thinkers are received in the global north – and like his preface to Fanon's *Wretched of the Earth*, the essay on Négritude should be taken with a pinch of salt: 'Black Orpheus' reduces the whole Négritude movement to Léopold Sédar Senghor and his *Anthologie de la nouvelle poésie nègre et malgache de langue française*

(Anthology of new black and Malagasy poetry in the French language; 1948). Sartre's preface was, in many ways, Négritude's

> kiss of death as it played an immense role in popularizing the Négritude movement and contributed to establishing Senghor's *Anthology* as its manifesto, but at the same time dismissed its historical significance by emphasizing that its being was ultimately only poetic, without real substance.[3]

Sartre, who was simultaneously Négritude's philosophical champion and its undertaker, forced the movement to define itself against his interpretation, and to defend its political and philosophical credibility against critiques that took the preface as a definite statement of its purpose. But could Négritude become more than the simple negation of white supremacy and turn towards the universal, as Sartre had hoped?

Unlike Senghor, Suzanne and Aimé Césaire and Léon Damas refused to extend Négritude into the realm of philosophy, or to claim that African cultures or religions possessed a unique African worldview.[4] In a lecture delivered at Florida International University in 1987, Aimé Césaire distanced himself from the metaphysical conflation of Blackness and Africanness. For Césaire, Négritude's intention was not to create a new metaphysics, philosophy or any other 'pretentious conception of the universe'. Rather, it was 'a way of living history within history: the history of a community whose experiences appears to be ... unique, with its deportation of old beliefs, its fragments of murdered cultures'.[5] Négritude, then, was simply the recognition that this shared history, which Césaire insisted had its own coherence, constituted a common Black heritage. But Césaire was hardly alone in advancing a 'thin' essentialism designed to counter racism in France and the Caribbean. In the 1943 essay 'Surrealism and Us', Suzanne Césaire gives a similar account of the political ambitions of her surrealism:

> So, far from contradicting, diminishing, or diverting our revolutionary feeling of life, surrealism shored it up. It nourished in us an impatient strength, endlessly sustaining this massive army of negations.
> And then I think also to tomorrow.
> Millions of Black hands, across the ranging clouds of world war, will spread terror everywhere. Roused from a long benumbing torpor, this most deprived of all people will rise up, upon plains of ashes.
> Our surrealism will then supply them the leaven from their very depths. It will be time finally to transcend the sordid contemporary antinomies: Whites-Blacks, Europeans-Africans, civilized-savage: the powerful magic of mahoulis will be recovered, drawn from the very wellsprings of life. Colonial idiocies will be purified by the welding arc's blue flame. The mettle of our metal, our cutting edge of steel, our unique communions – all will be recovered.[6]

For Aimé and Suzanne Césaire – and others involved in *Tropiques*, the journal they founded in 1941 alongside Georges Gratiant, Airstide Maugée, René Menil and Lucie Thesée – Négritude was a poetic revolt that sought to reclaim a heritage destroyed by slavery and colonisation. The Césaires belonged to a diaspora shaped by African, Atlantic and American histories of capture, commodification and enslavement. It was this common history which united Black people across the world; asserting a common identity, they argued, was precisely how to overcome the oppression and exploitation that had characterised the experiences of Black people throughout modern history. In their hands, Négritude transforms from a philosophical worldview into a political act directed at decolonisation.

The history of Négritude raises an important issue that has also been a recurring problem for the Western Marxist tradition: the alienation of radical or revolutionary intellectuals from the masses.[7] This is exacerbated in the case of intellectuals of the Black diaspora, as there is the additional element of alienation from a romanticised 'home'. Négritude – by its own admission – owes a huge debt to the Harlem Renaissance, which in principle is no problem at all. But when we consider Damas's claim that Négritude was founded on a 'wind rising from Black America' which expresses 'the African love for life, the African joy in love, [and] the African dream of death', we begin to realise how much our understanding of race in Africa is shaped by a diasporic standpoint.[8] In its early stages, Négritude thinking on Blackness was conditioned by both alienation from the revolutionary struggle – expressed in its emphasis on poetic and artistic revolt – and diasporic alienation, as intellectuals in the colonial metropole. One can spot such double alienation in contemporary ontological accounts of Blackness, as in AP 2.0's claim that Blackness is defined by 'natal alienation'.[9] Too often this perspective has drowned out and silenced analyses of race that take seriously the realities and material conditions of Black people on the African continent. Following Ali Mazrui, we might ask ourselves why this diasporic view

of Blackness ('Black Orientalism') is always applied glob-
ally and no attention is paid to the particularities of race
relations on the continent?[10]

But Aimé Césaire's attack on Roger Callois in *Discourse
on Colonialism* (1950), on the other hand, illustrates just
how ingrained the cultural exceptionalism of Europe was,
and still is, in many intellectuals' minds, and just how
necessary it was, and still is, to counter such exceptionalism with a 'thin' essentialism of one's own – even if this
expression is mainly poetic.[11] When we consider the infamous polemical open letter to Martinique's chief of information services that the editors of *Tropiques* published in
response to being censored and interdicted by the Vichy
regime, we get an even clearer picture of Négritude's
political purpose:

> Sir, we have received your indictment of *Tropiques*.
> 'Racists', 'sectarians', 'revolutionaries', 'ingrates and
> traitors to the country', 'poisoners of souls', none of
> these epithets really repulses us. 'Poisoners of souls',
> like Racine, 'ingrates and traitors to our good country',
> like Zola … 'revolutionaries', like the Hugo of
> 'Châtiments'. 'Sectarians', passionately, like Rimbaud
> and Lautrémont. Racist, yes. Of the racism of Toussaint
> Louverture, of Claude McKay and Langston Hughes
> against that of Drumont and Hitler. As to the rest of it,
> don't expect for us to plead our case, nor vain recrimi-
> nations, nor discussions. We do not speak the same
> language.[12]

Whereas we can read AP 2.0's essentialism as a retreat
from politics, the essentialism in Aimé Césaire's surrealism takes racism and colonialism head on. This 'strategic

essentialism' – a positivist essentialism that is critical of the ontological idea but uses it to achieve specific political gains – is somewhat at odds with the 'thick' ontological (and anti-political) Blackness promoted by AP 2.0 which has no political strategy whatsoever.[13] Nonetheless, we must remember that the emphasis in strategic essentialism is on political action. And while Négritude focused on deconstructing essentialism through poetry and art, a truly revolutionary Black politics must aim to engender a radical transformation of existing social relations. Both Senghor and Aimé Césaire's Négritude fed into a politics that was Francophile and increasingly distant from communism. And, as reductive as 'Black Orpheus' is, perhaps Sartre was right when he pointed to Négritude's political blind spots. Is it at all surprising that, under Césaire's leadership, Martinique chose to remain an overseas department of France?

Négritude's political failings are even more severe in the case of the African socialist government of the poet-turned-statesman Senghor. Senghor – who had called for a 'Negro African re-reading of Marx' – believed that African socialism would naturally develop out of African societies and cultures.[14] But his own African socialism was based on a particular reading of Marx: anticipating Louis Althusser's thesis of an epistemological break between early and late Marx, Senghor lamented Marx's transition from philosophy to the critique of political economy. While the *Grundrisse* or the three volumes of *Capital* positioned Marx as an anti-humanist thinker (which Althusser would praise), the *1844 Manuscripts* showed a Marx whose philosophical humanism was more relevant for the project of African socialism. As Diagne points out, Senghor thought the African rereading of Marx would 'save Marx the humanist, metaphysician, dialectician and artist from a narrowly materialist, economistic, positivist, realist Marxism' and 'invent an African path to socialism which was inspired by black spiritualities, and which continues the tradition of communism on the continent'. For Senghor, Marx's concept of alienation would provide the basis for liberation, as African people transcended both natural and sociopolitical alienation in the process of building African socialism.

While this might sound plausible at first, the move away from Marx's critique of political economy clears the path for the de-radicalised African socialism that would define the Senghor presidency of Senegal. Senghor, who was called a 'neo-colonial valet' by the Democratic Union of Senegalese Students (Union démocratique des étudiants du Senegal, UDES), was known to leftists in Senegal not as a hero of national liberation but as a close collaborator with French imperial interests in 'Françafrique'.[15] (Césaire was convinced that Senghor, at heart, loved and admired the French.) Since his student days in Paris in the late 1920s, Senghor had maintained a close relationship with Georges Pompidou, who would later serve as prime minister (1962–68) and president (1969–71) of France.[16] Pompidou's time in office coincided with Senghor's presidency (1960–80), and the latter would steer his newly independent nation into a position of continued political and economic dependency. But fostering such close ties with the French state required the repression of revolutionary politics, not least of the radical student movement; in the 1960s and '70s, radical left organisations had to survive in clandestine ways, and it was a legal offence to have revolutionary propaganda in one's possession. But Senghor's repression of political opposition also extended to comrades (former prime minister Mamadou Dia) and leftist parties, whose members were imprisoned, tortured or, in the case of Omar Blondin Diop, killed.[17]

Brent Hayes Edwards has detailed the emergence of Black internationalism in France during and after World War I, where 'African Americans, Antilleans and Africans were able to "link up"'.[18] But he also points to the challenges that Black people faced in trying to build international solidarity or, borrowing a phrase from Alain Locke, cast the 'race problem as a world problem'.[19] Edwards explains how attempts to organise among populations of African descent that reached beyond the barriers of language and nation were always 'necessarily skewed by those same boundaries'. A citizen of the United States, for example, had experienced a different form of racism and segregation than a 'French West African citizen marked by a context of colonialism'. Because the abstract use of diaspora flattens these differences – I'm thinking here of the conflation of Blackness and Africanness (Négritude and AP 2.0) or of Blackness and slavery (AP 2.0) – it might be more constructive to re-articulate the term (Blackness) to acknowledge how 'black groupings are fractured by nation, class, gender sexuality, and language'.[20] Edwards argues that we should develop a practice of Black internationalism that is attentive to the multiple histories of diaspora, and that reaches for linkages despite such differences. The bilingualism of the Black periodicals that were published in France and the US in the period after World War I provide an example for how we might build the institutional practices that make solidarity possible.

The Black bilingual journals of the interwar period can be contrasted with what I call a 'malpractice' of diaspora, i.e., the conflation of myriad experiences of racialisation under a monolithic Blackness. The Négritude of Senghor stands in contrast to the philosophy driving another, more militant Senghor, Lamine, a socialist and anti-imperialist organiser active in Paris and Marseille in the early twentieth century (the two were not related). Lamine Senghor was a member of the French Communist Party and one of the first to lead the Ligue de Défense de la Race Nègre (LDRN), an anti-imperialist organisation 'set up by Black Caribbeans and Africans during the 1920s and 1930s to unite men of the African and Black diaspora in their anti-French sentiment'.[21] Lamine pushed back against the exoticised portrayal of Black people in France, and organised workers based not only on race, but on their mutual experiences of exploitation. This was particularly important in a port city like Marseille, which unemployed or casually employed migrants from West and North Africa had made their (often temporary) home. Jennifer Boittin explains:

> Whereas Parisian Blacks demarcated themselves with racial terminology, and in particular whether they proudly considered themselves to belong under the traditionally negative term 'nègre' or preferred the more neutral denomination of 'noir', those in Marseille often described themselves by referring to their peoples of origin.[22]

As Tiemoko Garan Kouyaté – who took over the LDRN's organising in Bordeaux and Marseille after Lamine Senghor's death – soon found out, Black workers in Marseille resisted metropolitan views of Blackness that didn't reflect their own experiences as migrant workers in the multicultural Marseille.[23] Moreover, the league used 'seamen to distribute its publications throughout French West Africa' and the Caribbean and established a solid presence on the African continent.[24] This connected the movement's communist ambitions in France with its support for independence movements in West and Central Africa. Theirs was a Blackness that was revolutionary, international, and deeply rooted in the anti-colonial struggle – a practice of diaspora which allowed these Black intellectuals and organisers to build anti-imperialist solidarities that could confront racial capitalism in all its guises.

Yet the anti-colonial activists who form the political and intellectual tradition I call Red Africa flirted with Négritude, too. The Bissau-Guinean and Cape Verdean revolutionary Amílcar Cabral, for example, developed his politics through a critical engagement with Marxism *and* Négritude, alongside other students, while studying in Lisbon in the early fifties. Agostinho Neto, Mário Pinto de Andrade, Marcelino dos Santos and Cabral, who would all play crucial roles in their respective national-liberation movements, were *mestiço-assimilados*, belonging to a social class of colonial subjects considered 'civilised' enough to qualify for full rights as Portuguese citizens.[25] This, however, did not mean that they were part of a colonial elite; in fact, their families were often impoverished and competed for work with Portuguese immigrants who'd left their home country to find employment (more on this later). By providing scholarships, Portugal had hoped to shape African students into an elite that could staff parts of the colonial administration.

(Antonio Salazar's dictatorship had also taken to deporting 'troublesome' African students to Portugal.) Instead, they gathered at the Casa dos Estudiantes do Imperio (CEI) – a centre in Lisbon founded by white African-born students sympathetic to the Salazar regime – to discuss the future of Portugal's African colonies (or, more specifically, how to get rid of the Portuguese). They also became increasingly interested in Marxist ideas and established contact with Portuguese communists.

Cabral and his comrades embraced Négritude's positive affirmation of Blackness and African culture. But as they became more involved with the Portuguese Communist Party and the Soviet Union, their assessment of Négritude changed. Things came to a head when Santos, Andrade and his good friend Viriato da Cruz were invited to the First Conference of African and Asian Writers, which was held in Soviet Uzbekistan in 1958. The conference brought together 140 writers from thirty-six countries, including a ninety-year-old W.E.B. Du Bois, who flew in from Moscow. Andrade remembered the conference as a 'literary Bandung': a historic meeting of non-aligned writers that was not to be missed. But other African writers were unconvinced. In the lead-up to the conference, Alioune Diop, the Senegalese founder of the influential Paris-based journal *Présence Africaine*, expressed concerns about Soviet involvement, which he thought would distract from the focus on Black writing and art. When the Soviets refused to pull out, Diop and his journal boycotted the conference.[26] Andrade, who had joined *Présence Africaine* as an editor, was bitterly disappointed. Back in Lisbon, he'd been enamoured with the Négritude poetry of Césaire and Senghor – close collaborators of the journal – and considered the CEI the 'political home' of Portuguese Négritude. But the Tashkent conference showed that his politics had shifted to the left – he now considered Négritude too urban and bourgeois to be of any use in the anti-colonial struggle.[27]

Instead, the group turned to Marxism. They initially looked to the Soviet Union and Maoist China for ideological guidance and practical support. (Neto was the exception; he instead chose to align himself more closely with the Portuguese Communist Party.) Moscow was impressed with Cabral and Andrade, whom they considered potential recruits to their ideological cause. They shared Cabral's scepticism towards African socialism, the anti-colonial ideology espoused by Nkrumah, Sékou Touré and other African leaders (see chapter 6), for example. But official Soviet Marxism-Leninism had to contend with Maoism, whose peasant-based model of revolution appealed to the group. Maoist ideology and tactics provided the model for the zones set up in liberated areas in Guinea-Bissau and Mozambique during the independence war. It thus played a crucial role in ensuring the success of the anti-colonial struggle.[28] Neither ideology, however, prevented these anti-colonial activists from developing their own approach to Marxism, rooted in the histories of their respective nations. Theirs was a Marxism that, to borrow a phrase from Cabral, sought to 'return to the source' by connecting the insights of Marxian method with the conditions of struggle on the ground.[29] This creative approach to Marxism was characteristic of the political and intellectual tradition of Red Africa.

5

Whose Fanon? On Blackness and National Liberation

Frantz Fanon's political thought has become an indispensable resource for scholars and activists studying the effects of racism and colonialism in both the global north and global south. His work has even spawned its own field of enquiry, Fanon studies, which is dedicated to the various strands of his writing, ranging from early existentialist plays rooted in Césaireian Négritude to later psychiatric texts, and of course his infamous anti-colonial treatises. While most Fanon studies scholarship helps us better understand a complex figure who died too young – Fanon succumbed to leukaemia when he was only thirty-six – the discipline has also spawned some strange interpretations, or rather misreadings, of his oeuvre. There is, for example, the bizarre claim, made by AP 2.0, that we should draw a sharp distinction between Fanon as a thinker of Blackness and a postcolonial Fanon, or that only the 'Black/Slave' Fanon is the *true* Fanon and we should disregard his later anti-colonial writing. But this separation is not as clear-cut as scholars like Wilderson make it out to be.[1] The erasure of anti-colonial thought in AP 2.0, it seems, extends even to its most prized thinker. But we cannot grasp Fanon's intellectual and political development without considering him a thinker of *both* Blackness and national liberation.

The distinction between a Black/Slave Fanon and a postcolonial Fanon is based on a selective reading of certain passages of *Black Skin, White Masks* (1952), Fanon's first published book. Like Frank B. Wilderson III's *Afropessimism* (2020), *Black Skin* can be described as an autoethnography or a work of auto-theory (i.e., an attempt to create a philosophy by way of the self). Though Fanon is careful not to overstate his conclusion – he writes that since he 'was born in the Antilles [his] observations and . . . conclusions are valid only for the Antilles' – AP 2.0 elevates his account of anti-Black racism (as seemingly all-encompassing) to the level of universal truth. A closer consideration of the text in question, however, reveals something different. When he first moved from Martinique to Lyon, Fanon, who like the Négritude thinkers had been raised an *évolué*, saw himself not as a Black man, but as a Frenchman of Caribbean origin. But several encounters with racism – including the scene described in *Black Skin* where a child passes him crying out '*Maman*, look, a Negro; I'm scared!' – changed this self-identification.[2] Fanon realised that French society had developed in 'the Black' a desire for whiteness or, put simply, to belong to the realm of humanity. Yet no matter how well an educated, bourgeois Black person mastered the French language or culture, they could never truly be white. They would always be considered abnormal by racist French society.

At times, it might sound like Fanon is theorising Blackness as an eternal and *essentialist* category. But this isn't the case. In early plays such as *The Drowning Eye* and *Parallel Hands*, both written in 1949, 'whiteness and blackness are not absolute oppositions but relative, positional, on a scale of gradations'.[3] This is a Fanon who, as a Martinican, had experienced being treated as an 'honorary *tubab* – white man – not a native (*indigène*)', and who, as a 'quasi-metropolitan', was critical of any essentialist conception of Blackness.[4] Fanon knew that his experiences of Blackness in colonial Martinique weren't the same as in France. He was also keenly aware that his observations in *Black Skin* applied only to 'the Negro of the Antilles', and that a different text would have to be written about the experiences of 'the Negro of Africa'.[5] These variations in experience, he argues, also affect how we approach resistance to racism or colonialism in different contexts; there is, for example, a fundamental difference between the conditions and objectives of the US Civil Rights movement and Black anti-colonial struggle in Africa.[6] Yet this does not mean that nothing connects them. While Fanon often struggles to reconcile the two phases of his life, there is a sense of continuity in his work. Throughout his writing, he tries to come to terms with the complex legacies of European modernity, which folded colonised or Black people into its racial categories through slavery and colonialism. For Fanon, it is this legacy which links his experiences as a Black man in France to his later anti-colonial activism.

Fanon's early writing is characterised by a 'surrealist existentialism' inspired by his former teacher Aimé Césaire. His main influences at the time, apart from Césaire, were the existentialist philosophies of Kierkegaard, Nietzsche and Sartre, and the phenomenology of Maurice

Merleau-Ponty, whose lectures he had attended.[7] The transformation of the early Fanon into a theorist concerned with ontologies of Blackness rests almost entirely on a mistranslation and, consequently, misunderstanding of the title of the famous fifth chapter of *Black Skin*. 'The Fact of Blackness', which is not an ontological claim, is more accurately translated as 'The Lived Experience of the Black' ('L'expérience vécu du Noir'), making the chapter about the lived experience of Black people and not Black *being*. As Lewis Gordon explains, the term 'lived experience' was introduced to philosophy by Merleau-Ponty, who was searching for an accurate translation of the German word *Erlebnis*. This term should not be 'understood in English as "the objectively given or an event"', but as a 'process by which objects acquire their status as such for-consciousness'.[8] There is, then, no fact of Blackness as an ontological condition (in AP 2.0's sense of the term), but only the lived experience of being racialised as Black. The experience of racialisation creates the impression that Blackness is an inescapable and eternal condition; consequently, it transforms Blackness into a perceived reality.[9]

In a 1993 essay on 'The Appropriation of Frantz Fanon', Cedric J. Robinson already complained about the petit-bourgeois use of Fanon to justify 'post- or anti-revolutionary' intellectual projects.[10] There has been a deliberate effort to suppress the self-critique of the national bourgeoisie and the colonised intellectual that appears in Fanon's later work. Commenting on Robinson's essay, Gordon writes that Fanon was a revolutionary whose views are 'held suspect at the end of a century that began with the call to revolution ... and came to a close with antirevolutionary (if not counter-revolutionary) suspicion'.[11] Such counterrevolutionary suspicions are evident in the work of scholars like Henry Louis Gates Jr. or Wilderson, who present an imaginary purely psychonanalytic Fanon as the *only* true one. This blatant misuse of Fanon is a particularly infuriating example of how anti-colonial thought has been distorted by the neoliberal university and emptied of its revolutionary content. In reading parts of Fanon's early work selectively, disregarding later writings and ignoring his biography entirely, these scholars try to incorporate Fanon into their distorted genealogy of Black radicalism. And since *Black Skin, White Masks* makes for more comfortable reading for Black intellectuals in the US academy than *The Wretched of the Earth* (1961) or *A Dying Colonialism* (1959) – the more important texts for national liberation struggles on the continent – they have reached for the young Fanon and tried to isolate him from the rest of his oeuvre.

My aim here is not to offer a full account of Fanon's life and thought, but simply to push back against the narrow view of Black radicalism that overemphasises the importance of a bourgeois diaspora perspective, and that refuses to take seriously Fanon's (self-)critique of the 'native' or colonised intellectual. In *The Wretched of the Earth*, he explains that the native intellectual plays an important role in the process of decolonisation, but that their personal transformation differs from that of the peasant masses. At first, the intellectual suffers from a certain psychological condition that makes them identify with the oppressor; but during the liberation struggle, they begin to question the Western values that have been imprinted on their minds.[12] This allows the native intellectual to overcome mental reservations about the struggle, and encourages them to speak up for the cause of their people. But they are careful not to choose a side in the conflict between coloniser and colonised. Fanon criticises the intellectuals for being too easily persuaded by the colonial bourgeoisie who cite the common good as a valid reason to reject violent struggle. It is for this reason, Fanon argues, that the native intellectual cannot play a major role in the liberation struggle; the people, who remain sure of their objectives, will liberate themselves. This critical attitude towards the intellectual elite can be explained by his unease at the privilege of freedom which white society gives them while continuing to exploit their people. Fanon's later work can thus be read as an attempt to overcome this privilege and align himself with the oppressed.

The young Fanon, singled out and isolated from all other anti-colonial thought, has been granted a cushy place in the ivory tower. But why doesn't the same apply to Black revolutionaries such as Amílcar Cabral, one of the foremost anti-colonial theorists of the twentieth century? The academy's aversion to Cabral stems from its lack of interest in the crucial everyday work of revolutionary struggle and its fetishisation of revolution in the abstract. Cabral insisted that the revolution can never be separated from the daily needs of the people, and that we must not only fight the battle of ideas but struggle for material benefits and improved conditions of life. Instead of decontextualising Fanon, why not read him alongside other anti-colonial figures like Cabral who offer valuable insight into fields such as revolutionary strategy? Of course, this would mean that we would have to engage with *Toward the African Revolution* (1964), published anonymously while Fanon was writing for the Algerian National Liberation Front's (FLN) paper, *El Moudjahid*. These essays deal more directly with questions of neo-colonialism and imperialism, and begin to address revolutionary strategy and tactics. This Fanon insisted that the Algerian struggle for self-determination was proof that a new society could only be formed within the framework of national liberation.[13] He, too, deserves to be read.

But what was it about Algeria that led Fanon, a Black man from Martinique, to identify with it so closely? The plight of Algerians in France opened his eyes to how other racialised groups experienced everyday racism. In his psychiatric study on 'The North African Syndrome' (1952), Fanon analyses the mysterious illness tormenting North Africans in France. Building on Freud's concepts of phylogeny and ontogeny, Fanon develops a *sociogenic* approach to the neuroses and pathologies that afflict racialised or colonised subjects. While 'ontogenic approaches address the individual organism' and 'phylogenic approaches address the species', the sociogenic 'pertains to what emerges from the social world, the intersubjective world of culture, history, language and economics'.[14] By showing that these neuroses and pathologies were socially produced, not ontologically given, Fanon was challenging the racist prejudices of psychiatrists who dismissed these unexplained pains as imaginary illnesses. Taking the colonial construction of the North African as their starting point, they had glossed over the problems of 'alienated embodiment' which afflicted their patients. In fact, it was racist society that was making Algerians sick – and the psychiatric hospitals were only making things worse. Fanon soon realised that there could be no psychiatric treatment for problems of social alienation; only the total transformation of social relations would cure racialised and colonised subjects of their illness.[15]

We might also read Fanon's turn to Algeria through William Gardner Smith's novel *The Stone Face*, first published in 1963, a year after Algerian independence and two years after Fanon's death.[16] Smith's protagonist, Simeon Brown, a Black American man who loses an eye in a brutal racist attack early in the novel, has made his way to Paris to escape the urge to enact revenge by killing a white person. He arrives in a Paris we are all too familiar with from Black literary accounts, a Paris where Black Americans can seemingly escape the all-encompassing racism of the United States – as Baldwin put it, 'I could not hate the French, because they left me alone'. But earlier in the century, Claude McKay had already complained that 'the Negro intelligentsia [in Paris] is completely on the side of France', and this remains true in Smith's novel: the little group of expats is content to frequent the cafés of the Left Bank, paying little attention to the plight of other racialised people – especially 'les Arabes' – in the French capital.[17] For Simeon and his friends, Paris offers an antidote to the United States. Here, they can at last participate in the rituals of (white) bourgeois society. In any case, they are reluctant to support the Algerian struggle and would rather stay out of trouble.

French society is obviously still racist, just not toward Simeon and his group of émigré friends. When Simeon is involved in a fight after intervening in a sexual assault, he realises he is no longer the 'other' to the French. The officers let Simeon go while the Algerian man he fought is arrested. When the Algerian man, Hossein, sees Simeon the next day, he reminds Simeon that he is in a privileged position in France. ('Hey! How does it feel to be a white man? ... We're the niggers here!') Though Hossein keeps his distance at first, his friend Ahmed, a young Algerian medical student, takes a liking to Simeon. As Simeon begins to feel more connected to the Algerians in Paris, he tries to bring up their situation with his Black friends. They, however, brush aside any discussion of their privilege, claiming that 'Algerians are white people ... when they're with Negroes'. (There are parallels between this scene and Wilderson's story about his Palestinian friend Sameer, discussed in chapter 2.) Of course, the Algerians harbour prejudices of their own; in a debate with Simeon's girlfriend, a Polish concentration camp survivor, one of Ahmed's friends reveals his antisemitism, much to Simeon's dismay. But when two Algerian women tell him about the rape and torture committed by French soldiers in Algeria, he decides to join the struggle.

The Stone Face reaches its climax when Simeon joins an FLN-organised demonstration in Paris. What follows is a vivid description of the Paris massacre of 1961, where police murdered hundreds of Algerians and threw their bodies in the Seine. (*The Stone Face* is one of the first literary accounts of the massacre) As Adam Shatz points out, 'The original draft ... ended with Simeon heading to Africa, as his Algerian friends have urged him'.[18] But in the final version, he instead returns to the US to join the Civil Rights movement ('a battle harder than that of any guerrillas in any burnt mountains'). The academic Paul Gilroy has interpreted this ending as a retreat from anti-imperialist solidarity, and a 'capitulation to the demands of a narrow version of cultural kinship that Smith's universalizing argument appears to have transcended'.[19] But Shatz thinks there might be another way of interpreting the novel's ending: 'The Algerian struggle has not only given him the courage to confront the stone face he fled; it has transformed his understanding of American racism by inscribing it in a wider history of Western domination'. Yet this seems unconvincing considering that Smith, unlike his protagonist, had little interest in returning to the US, a country he strongly disliked. He instead chose to settle in Kwame Nkrumah's Ghana.

Like Smith, Fanon moved to Africa. He arrived in 1953, convinced that he could use his medical training to help Algerians fight their colonisers. He was initially employed at Blida-Joinville Hospital in Algiers to treat French soldiers who had tortured Algerians, as well as their victims.[20] But when the liberation war broke out, Fanon used the hospital grounds to train FLN combatants to become medics and nurses. He was expelled from Algeria in 1957 for his political activities, only to return to North Africa under a different name to join the FLN in Tunis. Later, as a member and representative of the provisional Algerian government in exile, he even supported them in acquiring medical supplies and guns by establishing supply lines across the Sahara. Fanon dedicated most of his later years to the Algerian cause. It was, for him, the beginning of a universal project that would liberate colonised peoples and allow them to undergo a process 'dis-alienation', so that they finally might be free.[21] Independence, he hoped, would produce the spiritual and material conditions for the emergence of a new, decolonised subject. But Fanon never got to witness the outcome of the liberation war (though it wasn't exactly what he'd hoped for).[22] He died in a hospital in the United States in 1961, only a few months before Algeria finally achieved its independence.

6

Neo-colonialism, or, The Emptiness of Bearing One's Flag

In the poem 'At Livingstone's Statue', Cheswayo Mphanza juxtaposes the image of his father's unmarked grave with the statue erected to honour the life and legacy of the Scottish colonialist David Livingstone at Victoria Falls, on the border between Zambia and Zimbabwe.[1] We follow the speaker as they find Livingstone's statue and greet him with the same words the fellow colonialist Henry Morton Stanley supposedly uttered when he found an ill and dying Livingstone in Ujiji on Lake Tanganyika ('Dr. Livingstone, I presume?'). But the speaker isn't here to save Livingstone's life; instead, they want to crack the statue with a hammer and shatter 'Mason jars of piss' against Livingstone's face. The poem evokes the tension between the historical event of decolonisation and the colonial symbols and structures which persist in formally independent nations. There is a feeling of 'emptiness in bearing one's flag'. How much, Mphanza asks, has really changed for most Zambians since Kenneth Kaunda became the first president of the independent state? What does independence really mean if colonial relations still govern the lives of most Zambians who, like the speaker's father, are relegated to unmarked graves while Livingstone's statue still stands?

Though Bandung-era politics had promised to liberate the people of the Third World from imperialism, the outcome was something quite different. The emergence and spread of neoliberalism, and the re-integration of Bandung nations into a new imperial order led by the United States, undermined their ability to deliver on the promises of national liberation (see chapter 1). Of course, imperialist states, multinational companies and international organisations all played a role in crafting the neo-colonial state, as Kwame Nkrumah famously explained in *Neo-Colonialism: The Last Stage of Imperialism*.[2] But the transformation of African states into neo-colonies also required a compliant elite who would embrace the language of the nation while remaining loyal to the objectives of the imperialist bourgeoisie. While this new neo-colonial elite profited handsomely from the new arrangement, working people across the continent, many of whom had fought for independence, were left empty-handed. As the Ghanaian novelist Ayi Kwei Armah succinctly put it in his 1968 novel *The Beautyful Ones Are Not Yet Born*, 'The only real gain . . . for which poor men had fought and shouted [was] not that the whole thing be overturned and ended, but that a few blackmen might be pushed closer to their masters, to eat some of the fat into their bellies too'.[3]

Debates about the crisis of the postcolonial African state have recently been reignited by scholars like Mahmood Mamdani and Michael Neocosmos who have tried to understand why these states have failed to deliver on the promises of national liberation.[4] The complexities of each position are beyond us here, but it is worth noting

a shared concern with the possibility of a truly democratic and emancipatory politics in Africa (understood
not as the liberal project of legitimising class rule but the
plan to strengthen independent forms of organisation and
community solidarity which might help working people
hold neo-colonial regimes accountable). The late
Congolese scholar Ernest Wamba dia Wamba argued
that the unravelling of national liberation was the result
of a failure to democratically empower popular forces
that could challenge the state and the party. Instead, anti-
colonial leaders crowned themselves the 'new pharaohs
of . . . independent countries' by presenting themselves as
the personification of the country's national aspirations.[5]
In his assessment of the Mozambican anti-colonial struggle, John Saul similarly claims that its de-radicalisation
can be explained by the weakness of democratic institutions which should help the people 'understand and act
upon their class interests'.[6] But what led movements that
had once been the champions of national liberation to
turn towards authoritarianism?

The term 'African socialism' first emerged in the wake of
the independence struggles of the 1950s and '60s, when
newly independent governments sought to create the
basis for a new future, and once and for all break with the
racial, political and economic legacies of colonialism.
There is much debate around the definition of African
socialism, and many still argue – as the editors of the
1979 volume *Socialism in Sub-Saharan Africa* did in their
introduction – that the 'passage of time has not led to a
precise definition' or 'a general consensus on its nature'.[7]
Most scholars do agree, however, that African socialism

– as a political and intellectual tradition – can be split into two relatively distinct phases: a first wave of humanist African socialism and a second, more radical wave of Marxist-inspired movements more attuned to the principles of scientific socialism. This is, of course, a simplification, since the definition given here cannot capture the nature of all socialist anti-colonial movements. But this distinction can help us discern a particular set of themes that were developed within these currents, to better understand their aims, contradictions and limitations.

The humanist wave of African socialism dominates both academic discourse and the popular imaginary. The socialist projects of Kwame Nkrumah in Ghana, Julius Nyerere in Tanzania, Sékou Touré in Guinea, Kenneth Kaunda in Zambia, Léopold Senghor in Senegal and Modibo Keïta in Mali are some of the more prominent examples. Their anti-colonial politics were inspired by Nasserism – which had laid the foundations for non-alignment – and their socialism was based on the conviction that traditional communal elements of African culture were inherently socialist, and could serve as the basis for an egalitarian programme of national development. (Keïta, who remained committed to official Marxism–Leninism, was the exception.) The first wave of African socialism drew its inspiration from ideas first articulated by the Négritude poets. As Robin D.G. Kelley explains, Césaire's claim that 'pre-colonial African and Asian cultures were not only ante-capitalist . . . but also anti-capitalist' prefigures African socialism's romantic notion of a socialism founded on 'pre-colonial village life'.[8] But this first wave of African socialism fell short of delivering the radical promises made at independence. Attempts to create idealist humanisms, such as Nyerere's *ujamaa* socialism or Kaunda's 'Zambian humanism', only served to mask class relations in independent nations. Though they appealed to socialism as a source of political legitimacy, their ideological commitments were weak. Often, the idea of a 'pre-colonial' socialism, emptied of its revolutionary content, was used to silence a leftist opposition which sought to challenge the one-party state by evoking a different, more radical kind of Marxian socialism.

Though Kenya never moved beyond what Samir Amin has called a 'banal neocolonial framework', its early post-colonial history is nonetheless instructive here. As independence approached, the UK and the US had chosen Jomo Kenyatta as the preferred leader of an independent Kenya. But to succeed in installing a pro-imperialist government, Kenyatta had to sell imperialist positions to the public as 'authentically African and therefore most appropriate'.[9] This was accomplished through the Sessional Paper No. 10 titled *African Socialism and Its Application to Planning in Kenya*, which used the language of African socialism to define a project of national development that relied heavily on private capital and ensured that the country's economy continued to focus on the export of primary commodities. The purpose of the paper was to remove the terms capitalism and socialism from public discourse, and to establish a dependent economy: 'Kenyatta [even] made it clear in his introduction . . . that the intent was not to stimulate discussions on Kenya's economic policy, but to end it'.[10] More importantly, as Kenyatta himself admitted, the document was supposed to usher in the 'end of ideology' in Kenya (i.e., to cast aside ideological differences that threatened national unity and stability). Because no class problem existed in traditional African society, the document's co-author Tom Mboya argued, Marxism was irrelevant in Kenya. (Mboya, it later transpired, was in close contact with the CIA.) After independence, he further claimed, African socialism would avert the rise of antagonistic social classes by 'Africanising' the economy.[11] There was no need, then, for Marxism – and even less for communism – which was portrayed as alien and un-African.

The erasure of leftist opposition wasn't only ideological. 'The end of radicalism' – a phrase used by the historian Wunyabari O. Maloba to describe Kenyatta's elimination of the leftist opposition between 1963 and 1978 – refers to the violent and almost complete elimination of any radical socialist opposition by post-independence govern-ments on the continent.[12] Maloba's phrase forces us to reconsider the counterrevolutionary projects which sought to end conflicts about political ideology and fuse party, state and nation in the one-party state. Shortly before the Sessional Paper No. 10 was to be tabled, Jaramogi Oginga Odinga, the leader of the socialist wing in the Kenya African National Union (KANU), and the Goan-Kenyan MP Pio Gama Pinto were preparing a competing paper which would reject the government's proposal and call for a vote of no confidence in Kenyatta.[13] The opposition faction around Odinga had argued that independence must mean a total break with colonialism; they were, of course, dissatisfied with the sessional paper's articulation of a subservient capitalist economy in post-independence Kenya. To ensure that there would be no further conflict, Pinto – who was described by the last colonial governor of Kenya, Malcolm MacDonald, as 'a dedicated Communist, and the principal brain behind the whole secret organisation of Odinga's movement' – had to be eliminated.[14] He was shot dead in broad daylight outside his home in February 1965.

At the heart of the sessional paper was the language of African socialism as developed by Julius Nyerere, the first post-independence president of Tanzania, in his *ujamaa* (familyhood, in Swahili) socialism. By seeking a 'third way socialism' somewhere between the two poles of the Cold War's participants, Nyerere sought to build on the Non-Aligned Movement, and to break with foreign domination. In the Arusha Declaration of 1967, which proclaimed that Tanzania was officially a socialist state, he made a firm commitment to supporting African liberation movements. This allowed him to present himself as a radical leader of national liberation.[15] But this image obscured his involvement in suppressing his leftist opponents at home. Nyerere had worked with the US and the UK to make sure that the islands of Zanzibar wouldn't fall into the hands of communists following a revolution which overthrew the sultan in 1964.[16] Though Marxists like A.M. Babu had tried to lead the revolution in a communist direction, Zanzibar's new president, Abeid Karume, tended towards moderation, and eventually agreed to form a union between Zanzibar and Tanganyika (as Tanzania) with Nyerere as president.

Karume was appointed as Nyerere's vice president. Babu and his comrades were increasingly sidelined and excluded from influential government positions. In 1972, Karume was assassinated, and Babu and other former members of the communist Umma Party were put on trial and charged with treason for their alleged involvement. Babu was imprisoned on the Tanzanian mainland for five years. In prison, Babu wrote *African Socialism or Socialist Africa*, a scathing critique of Nyerere's *ujamaa* socialism.

The book was a passionate call for a mass-based, democratic socialism rooted in the social and economic realities
of Zanzibar. Like Amílcar Cabral, he emphasised the
development of national productive forces, arguing that
the profits from agricultural products like cloves should be
used to develop other industries that would make the
country less reliant on primary commodity exports.
Moreover, before unification Babu had been working on
trilateral trade arrangements with countries like Indonesia
and East Germany who would provide Zanzibar with the
machinery to develop its industries. Babu strongly disagreed with what he considered Nyerere's disastrous
economic policies, which had failed to generate prosperity.
African socialism, for Babu, simply meant the centralisa-
tion of economic power and the penetration of government and party into the economy, as well as the repression
of alternative political and economic visions. As Amrit
Wilson explains, 'The key slogan was self-reliance', but it
was really 'much more about austerity and control'.[17]

The Guyanese activist-scholar Walter Rodney arrived
in Tanzania in 1969 after being banned from re-entering
Jamaica, where he had been teaching. In Tanzania,
Rodney joined the University of Dar es Salaam, a hotbed
of Third Worldist radicalism, and worked on putting
together *How Europe Underdeveloped Africa*. He also
contributed to the revolutionary student magazine *Cheche*
and got involved in Tanzanian politics. But, as Leo Zeilig
points out, he 'was acutely aware of his role as a guest'.[18]
Though he understood that Tanzania was poor and
underdeveloped, Rodney broadly supported Nyerere's
ujamaa state until the early seventies. He was critical but
optimistic that there was some value in Nyerere's state-
led socialist project. In a 1972 article, for example,

Rodney distinguished *ujamaa* from Senghor's Négritude-inspired African socialism, arguing that the former was a more serious attempt at improving the lives of the peasant population, and a 'more decisive break with capitalism'.[19] But Nyerere's repression of opposition leaders, foreign dissenters and student activists began to worry him. The growth of the government bureaucracy, which was increasingly trying to influence every aspect of social, political and economic life, was also concerning. Rodney, who left Tanzania in 1974 to return to Guyana, where he was assassinated in 1980, eventually became disillusioned with Nyerere. He admitted that *ujamaa* had 'failed to live up to certain types of expectations'.[20]

Yet this narrative of betrayal is complicated by the contradictory positions that many African socialist leaders held, especially regarding nonalignment and the need for class analysis. Let's take Nkrumah as an example. At one point, he called for a position of nonalignment by claiming, 'We face neither East nor West; we face forward'.[21] But in *Revolutionary Path* (1973), he argues, 'If we are to achieve revolutionary Socialism, then we must avoid any suggestion that will imply there is any separation between the Socialist World and a "Third World"'.[22] *Class Struggle in Africa*, first published in 1970, also shows a Nkrumah deeply concerned with analysing how the close links of class and race developed in Africa alongside capitalist exploitation. He writes:

Slavery, the master-servant relationship, and cheap labour were basic to it. The classic example is South Africa, where Africans experience double exploitation – both on the ground of colour and class. Similar conditions exist in the US, the Caribbean, in Latin

America, and in other parts of the world where the
nature of the development has resulted in a racist class
structure. In these areas, even the shades of colour
count – the degree of blackness being a yardstick by
which social status is measured.[23]

In the colonial situation, a racist social structure cannot
be thought separately from class exploitation and a racist-
capitalist power structure. For Nkrumah, capitalist
exploitation and racism are complementary ('wherever
there is a race problem it has become linked with the class
struggle'); therefore, genuine progress in the struggle
against racism can only be made if intellectuals engage
Marxism and other communist organisations that encourage close contact with workers and peasants. In short,
African socialists must align themselves with the oppressed
masses and become conscious of the class struggle in
Africa.

In a comparison of the 1964 and 1970 editions of
Nkrumah's book *Consciencism*, the Beninese philosopher
Paulin Hountondji makes the convincing argument that
his thought developed towards class analysis and an even
more sober analysis of neo-colonialism after the 1966
US-backed military coup (Nkrumah's government was
overthrown while he was out of the country on a state
visit to North Vietnam and China).[24] In the 1964 edition,
Nkrumah praised the socialist elements inherent in
African traditional culture, but in the 1970 edition he
was more cautious with such claims. This shift of emphasis is also strikingly clear in his 1967 paper 'African
Socialism Revisited', where he criticises African socialists
who have associated it 'much more with anthropology
than political economy' and fetishised African communal

life by deluding themselves that it was devoid of social hierarchy. Following the military coup, Ghana cultivated a closer relationship with the US – and, of course, with associated 'international' organisations like the World Bank and the IMF – and cut ties with the Soviet Bloc. Even last-ditch attempts by Soviet intelligence to bring Nkrumah back from exile in Guinea and restore his government could not save Ghana from taking its assigned (dependent) place in the imperial order.

The military coup in Ghana is a key scene in the autobiography of Maryse Condé, one of the foremost literary voices of the French Caribbean. Condé, who was born in the French overseas department of Guadeloupe in 1937, was raised by parents who had ascended to the island's embryonic Black petit bourgeoisie (who call themselves 'les Grands Nègres').[25] When Condé leaves for Paris aged sixteen, she is destined for a bright future. But like the Négritude poets and Fanon, she discovers that the metropole isn't exactly what she'd expected; here, she can never truly be French. Following an unexpected pregnancy and the death of her mother, Condé falls into an ever more precarious financial situation. Her life as part of the privileged Black bourgeoisie has come to an end, and she begins to distance herself from the Antillean *évolués,* who identify as bourgeois Frenchmen, instead spending more time among the 'Africans'.

In 1958, Condé marries her first husband, the Guinean actor Mamadou, convinced that marriage will restore her social status. But it is a marriage of convenience, and she soon realises that it is bound to fail. Inspired by Césaireian Négritude, she makes her way to the Ivory Coast in the hope that it might finally provide an escape from her husband, the Antilles and her miserable life in Paris. For a twenty-year-old Condé, Africa is not yet a real place – it is merely a dream inspired by the literary imaginary of her fellow Antillean poets. But the reality is different: Condé is at first shocked by the poverty and destitution of the mass of people in the Ivory Coast. She also notices the tension between her fellow Antilleans and Ivorians, shattering any remaining hopes of a unified and monolithic Blackness that might bind people of African descent together.[26]

After Condé decides to tell Mamadou that she has secretly had his child, he invites her to join him in Guinea. But she is disappointed by the African socialism of Sékou Touré, Guinea's first post-independence president. At the time, Guinea was considered a beacon of anti-colonial resistance; it was the only French-speaking country in Africa to have voted against adopting the new French constitution, which would have made Guinea an overseas department, a state within the French community, or an overseas territory. Guinea also rejected the offer to keep the CFA franc; instead, it created its own central bank and printed its own currency, the Guinean franc. But Condé shows us a different side of Touré. She remembers him driving his Mercedes along the coast as poor fishermen cheer him on, which doesn't sit quite right with her. Wasn't African socialism supposed to benefit *all* the people? Recalling Fanon's 'The Pitfalls of National Consciousness' in *The Wretched of the Earth*, she writes that the chapter seems to have been written 'expressly for Guinea', where the 'architects of revolution [had] gradually [become] its gravediggers'.[27]

Condé's autobiography documents the counterrevolution that put an end to the hopes of national liberation.

Following the coup in Ghana, where Condé was living at the time, she is deported for her suspected ties to Guinea, whose president, Touré, had offered Nkrumah the co-presidency. When she returned to Ghana in 1967, everything had changed: 'I toured the town', she writes, 'but didn't recognize it'.[28] Moreover, 'game shows and insipid American series' had replaced Nkrumah's speeches about colonialism on television. 'Is this progress?' she asked herself. This new Ghana, she concludes, is the Ghana of people like her former partner Kwame Aidoo, a sophisticated, Oxford-educated lawyer from a noble family of Ghanaian chiefs. Condé had returned to the world of *les Grands Nègres* that she'd so desperately tried to escape.

7
Remnants of Red Africa

The second wave of African socialism – or what is sometimes called Afro-Marxism – emerged from the mid-1970s onwards, though the period of preparation for the anti-colonial struggle began much earlier. This second phase of socialism was characterised by adherence to the principles of official Marxism-Leninism (with a vanguard party that leads the way to revolution) in countries like Burkina-Faso, Congo-Brazzaville, Madagascar, Libya, Benin and Ethiopia, though many of these were more militaristic in character than revolutionary.[1] The most radical among this wave, however, were the national liberation struggles in the Portuguese colonies: revolutionary movements that sought to overthrow the existing social structures and refashion these along socialist lines. The most influential proponents of this form of Afro-Marxism include: Amílcar Cabral (Guinea-Bissau and Cape Verde), Agostinho Neto and Mário Pinto de Andrade (Angola), and Marcelino dos Santos, Eduardo Mondlane and Samora Machel (Mozambique). In her autobiography, Condé, a fierce critic of the supposed heroes of national liberation, speaks highly of figures like

Andrade and Cabral, both whom she met in Conakry in the 1960s: 'If I became a Marxist, it was thanks to their contact rather than personal reasoning'.[2] Along with Pinto, Babu, Condé, and Andrée Blouin, they form the political and intellectual tradition I call Red Africa.

Anti-colonial movements in the Portuguese colonies in Africa were radicalised by the realities of the Portuguese dictatorship and its continued economic reliance on the colonies, not only as sources of raw materials and labour, but as sites of emigration for its own impoverished working class. The peculiar class dynamics in colonial Mozambique, for example, can only be understood in connection with the economic and political situation in Portugal itself. In the early sixties, Portugal had one of the lowest per capita incomes in Europe and a stagnant rate of economic growth. Moreover, the country had few natural resources, little industry, a shortage of land, difficulties with overpopulation and a large unemployed or underemployed surplus population. To compensate, Portugal decided to advertise the colonies as an emigration outlet for its mass of poor and unemployed workers. This created an atypical class structure within the 'overseas territories': large parts of the white settler population competed directly with Africans for 'low-skilled' work, but received preferential treatment and earned significantly higher wages for the same tasks.[3] Of course, wages were based on racial considerations, and they were often so low that they were insufficient to keep the worker alive.[4] Therefore, it was common practice among Black workers to engage in subsistence farming alongside wage labour to supplement their meagre income.

Portuguese colonialism claimed to have no racial bias.[5] This claim was based on the idea of *lusotropicalism*, which claimed that people of Portuguese background were preordained to lead the world toward racial harmony by building a far-flung empire composed of peoples of various colours, religions and linguistic groups.[6] The Portuguese claim to colour blindness was also underpinned by a policy of assimilation: the 'civilised' African who could 'speak Portuguese, had divested himself of all tribal customs and was regularly and gainfully employed' was, by law, a full Portuguese citizen, whereas other 'unassimilated' Africans were subject to the rule of a colonial administration.[7] Mozambique was officially divided into subgroups according to different 'socioeconomic strata'. Although there were a few *assimilado* Africans and *mestiço* among the group of higher economic standing, the lower economic groups were almost entirely composed of those categorised as 'Black' Africans. Forced labour, too, was common in Portuguese colonies, and different legal codes were applied to racialised Africans to ensure the coexistence of both white free labour and Black forced labour in the colonial economy.[8] But regardless of the legal codification, the fundamental relationship was the same: Black Mozambicans were a resource to be exploited for the benefit of Portugal.

Because Portugal's colonies were used as an emigration outlet for its own population, the local petit bourgeoisie became increasingly redundant, which led to their radicalisation and closer identification with the masses. Cabral, for example, came from this class and used his work for the colonial administration to plan and prepare the independence war (and to become part of what he later called the revolutionary petit bourgeoisie). This petit bourgeois class had emerged from relations of slavery and colonisation that were peculiar to the Cape Verde archipelago. Cape Verde, which lies around 570 kilometres off the West African coast, was first populated by Portuguese, Genoese, Castilians, Jews and enslaved Africans who worked on the islands' plantations. Later, with the rise of the transatlantic slave trade and a decline in productivity on the plantations, it became an entrepot for the transport of enslaved Africans to Mexico, Peru and Brazil. The island's demographic makeup changed and a multiracial population emerged which eventually came to dominate the island (due in part to the arrival of Portuguese runaways who settled there).[9] When the economy of the islands collapsed after the abolition of the transatlantic slave trade, many Cape Verdeans emigrated to different parts of the Portuguese colonial empire, later making up large parts of the *assimilado* class occupying the lower tiers of the colonial administration.

Cabral had studied agronomy in Lisbon, and his class position allowed him to take frequent trips across Guinea-Bissau, not only to study its social structure and soil – he conducted its first agricultural census – but to assess Bissau-Guineans readiness for the liberation war. Cabral had vowed to 'mobilize and organize the peasant masses', whom he considered the 'principal physical force of the national liberation struggle', but pressure from the Portuguese secret police (PIDE) forced him into exile.[10] He settled in Conakry, the capital of Touré's Guinea, where he set up the headquarters of the Party for the Independence of Guinea and Cape Verde (PAIGC). Cruz and Andrade, too, had made their way to Conakry in search of a base for the exiled Popular Movement for the Liberation of Angola (MPLA). From Guinea, Cabral and the PAIGC began to organise the liberation war; by 1968, the PAIGC had managed to liberate over two-thirds of the territory of Guinea-Bissau.[11] The 'liberated zones', areas freed through military action, formed a de facto independent state before the country officially gained independence. For Cabral, military action was a means for protecting civilian activities in the liberated areas, and the PAIGC tried to hold militants accountable in areas where crimes had been committed against the local population.[12] The liberated zones formed a people-led state within a state, complete with schools, medical posts and judicial and administrative structures. They expressed a vision of decolonisation that reached beyond a minimalist conception of the nation-state.

This was the case in Mozambique, too. As Aquino de Bragança and Jacques Depelchin have suggested, the ideological character of the Liberation Front of Mozambique (Frelimo) may have been closer to a truly revolutionary Marxism during the period of the liberated zones than when it was officially institutionalised as a vanguard party of peasants and workers.[13] During the liberation war, Frelimo experimented with radically different socioeconomic relations and institutions in the zones that had been liberated through military action and where popular democratic structures were established that could form the basis of a future independent Mozambique. And although these transformations did not reach the same level on all fronts – and despite their militaristic nature – they were important sites for democratic experimentation. In the liberated zones, Frelimo encouraged a complete transformation of social and economic relations through a combination of the most useful elements of both 'traditional' and revolutionary culture. The party's cadres not only brought elements of their own cultures with them to the camps, they also 'learned those of others, while in the fields of production new ideas and techniques [were] being introduced both from different areas of Mozambique and outside'.[14] This led to the growth of entirely new political structures, which gestured towards a postcolonial society that would change people's lives in fundamental ways.[15]

Yet much of what we know about the liberated zones in both Mozambique and Guinea-Bissau is derived from accounts of the anti-colonial leaders themselves or the journalists, photographers and filmmakers they invited to help spread PAIGC and Frelimo propaganda.[16] These accounts tend to leave out some of the more complicated aspects of the guerrilla war and life in the liberated zones. Of course, ethnic tensions hadn't disappeared entirely, and the Portuguese made use of these to destroy what Cabral called 'the political and moral unity of our people'.[17] Cabral had envisioned that Guinea-Bissau and Cape Verde, two countries with vastly different histories, social structures and ethnic compositions, be liberated together under the banner of the PAIGC. But the armed struggle was only taking place in Guinea-Bissau. As Antonio Tomas points out, this meant that the party's military units were mostly composed of Bissau-Guineans. Moreover, the country's civilian population had to bear the brunt of the war.[18] This led to tension between combatants and the 'privileged' Cape Verdean leadership, which would never be resolved. There was also the issue of Cabral leading the war from exile in Guinea. An effective Portuguese counterinsurgency campaign put the People's Revolutionary Armed Forces (FARP) under severe pressure, but Cabral was often absent from the frontlines of the struggle. This negatively affected the morale of PAIGC cadres and, Tomas suggests, created 'enough justification for a conspiracy against Cabral's leadership'.[19]

Their cosmopolitan backgrounds and socioeconomic standing as urban *mestiço-assimilado* intellectuals often put leaders like Cabral or Mondlane at odds with cadres from rural areas. Like the MPLA, Frelimo was dominated by a leadership that had enjoyed access to educational and socioeconomic opportunities that were off-limits to most Mozambicans. This was a persistent cause of conflict in the organisation, which 'was highly fractured from the start'.[20] Party cadres and students who objected to Mondlane's leadership and Santos's role in drafting the party's Marxist-Leninist constitution were mostly ethnic Makonde from the poorer, northern parts of the country who'd taken Maoism as their model for revolutionary action. (Makonde nationalist organisations had first emerged in exile in the 1950s, when they'd moved to British East Africa to escape forced labour in colonial Mozambique. Maoism became a popular ideology among anti-colonial activists based in Dar es Salaam, where Nyerere's *ujamaa* socialism echoed its slogans of 'self-reliance, hard work ... and rural transformation'.) In March 1968, students at the Mozambique Institute – set up by Mondlane and his wife, Janet, to train Frelimo cadres – revolted and demanded the removal of white professors and the party leadership. Mondlane eventually subdued the rebellion, but it severely impacted his ability to lead the liberation movement.

Cabral, too, had to deal with student revolt in the ranks of the PAIGC. Many African students had become disillusioned with communism after experiencing racist attacks – including the murder of a Ghanaian – while studying in the Eastern Bloc. Several students on PAIGC-sponsored scholarships took part in the wave of anti-racist protests that took Moscow (and Cabral) by surprise. But their criticism was not only directed at the Soviets; in fact, it was directed at the *mestiço-assimilado* leadership of the PAIGC and the MPLA, including Cabral and Neto. Both parties responded by suspending the students' scholarships and launching a campaign against the Maoist alliance within the Federation of African Students, which had become their preferred outlet for discontent. China's anti-Soviet tactics were seemingly working; in Tanzania, for example, the TANU Youth League, which had modelled itself after the Red Guards, was spreading anti-Soviet propaganda. Even Kwame Nkrumah, the elder statesman of African socialism, had shifted towards a pro-China position. But Cabral, who'd become increasingly critical of Nkrumah's politics, refused to cut off the Soviets, which caused a breakdown in relations between China and the PAIGC. But Maoist intervention led to the opposite of the outcome Beijing had hoped for: power was now firmly concentrated around the pro-Soviet Cabral and Neto.

Cabral's pro-Soviet position didn't mean he uncritically embraced orthodox Marxism-Leninism. Examples of Cabral's innovative approach to Marxist theory are, of course, his concepts of the 'nation-class' and 'class suicide'.[21] Despite his sharp criticism of the neo-colonial bourgeoisie, he believed that the petit bourgeoisie could play a crucial role in the nationalist struggle against direct colonial occupation. Cabral had determined that the main class contradiction in colonial society was between the internal and external supporters of imperialism and the masses as a nation-class. He thus saw the potential for revolution in an alliance of various social classes, including the peasantry and the petit bourgeoisie. For Cabral, there were three stages in the anti-colonial revolution. First, there would be the revolution of the nation-class against colonialism. Second, class differences would emerge or become more visible in postcolonial society. Third, there would be a socialist revolution within the revolution, through which the masses would work to eradicate class differences. This third step, however, required the petit bourgeois vanguard of the independence movement to commit class suicide – to sacrifice its privilege through identification with the masses.[22] If this did not happen, the revolution would deteriorate into authoritarian statism or state capitalism.

For Cabral, national liberation movements faced a zero-sum choice at independence: neo-colonialism or socialism. Under neo-colonialism, imperialist action takes on the form of creating a native bourgeoisie that is loyal to the bourgeoisie of the imperialist nations.[23] Their loyalty to the imperialist bourgeoisie stifles the development of national productive forces, and inevitably leads to underdevelopment. Therefore, this class cannot guide the development of productive forces, and cannot be a truly national bourgeoisie. Under neo-colonialism, the struggle for the 'independent' state (and political power) is thus between the native working class and imperialist capital. Because neo-colonial societies are structures along vertical lines, it is difficult to build a cross-class coalition or a united front against imperialist domination. The material and psychological effects of the emergence of sharp class distinctions demobilise the nationalist forces, and enable ethnic ties to make their way back to the forefront of politics. The class of workers and their allies (i.e., the agricultural proletariat and the peasantry) are now forced to fight both the native and the imperialist bourgeoisie, as class struggle becomes the dominant mode of politics. Yet this national class struggle is precisely where the anti-imperialist revolution begins: with the destruction of capitalist structures 'implanted in the national soil'.[24]

The liberation war in Portuguese Africa was, nonetheless, shaped by the politics of the Cold War. Mondlane had met Santos, the co-founder of Frelimo, in Lisbon in the fifties when Cabral and Neto were also in town. Like Neto, Mondlane was harassed by PIDE, which made life in Portugal so difficult that he eventually left for the US (an unusual move for Africans from Portuguese colonies) to study at Oberlin College and Northwestern University (he briefly taught at Harvard and Syracuse, too). When he arrived in Dar es Salaam, Mondlane had already established an international network of high-level contacts, including former colleagues from his time with the UN.[25] But some cadres in Frelimo distrusted Mondlane because of close ties to the United States.[26] In 1963, Mondlane had approached Robert Kennedy in hopes of securing funding for Frelimo. Kennedy was impressed with Mondlane and offered him $60,000 through the Ford Foundation, which was closely linked to the CIA.[27] Nonetheless, Mondlane skilfully utilised 'Dar es Salaam's position at the epicentre of international politics in sub-Saharan Africa to attract material aid and public support'.[28] When it came to negotiating with Moscow, however, it was Santos, who had formed a close relationship with the Soviets and various European communist parties, who was most useful.

The PAIGC relied on assistance from the Soviet Union, Cuba and Czechoslovakia to acquire weapons, military training and cash to fund their guerrilla war. In return, they hoped to get information on the development of (and political conflicts within) the national liberation movements in Africa and across the Third World. When Nkrumah was exiled to Guinea, 'Czechoslovak Intelligence used the relationship with Cabral to better understand Nkrumah's plans in order to influence his decision-making process'.[29] Following the first conference of the Non-Aligned Movement, in Belgrade in 1961, they sought to gain 'information on a wide range of issues, such as divisions among the delegates, and their views of nonalignment, the German question and Soviet Bloc policy in Africa', though Cabral didn't give them much to work with.[30] (It is likely that he didn't know he had been recruited and classified as a 'clandestine contact'.) While the Soviets and the Warsaw Pact states were sometimes disillusioned with the potential for socialism in Africa, they nonetheless continued to support Cabral and the PAIGC. By the time the liberation war broke out in 1963, Cabral had established a 'transnational support network, which included supporters in Ghana, Algeria, Morocco, Czechoslovakia, Cuba and the Nordic countries'. Cabral, then, was able to pragmatically use the intensification of the Cold War to obtain international support and further the PAIGC's cause.

The Carnation Revolution accelerated the breakup of the Portuguese Empire in Africa. On April 24, 1974, the Armed Forces Movement (MFA) – an organisation of low-ranking officers with leftist sympathies in the Portuguese Armed Forces – launched a coup which quickly transformed into a popular movement for democracy.

The fall of the dictatorship and the success of the anti-colonial struggle were intimately connected. As Perry Anderson noted in 1962, over a decade before the revolution, the regime was utterly dependent on the existence of its colonies and would not survive their independence.[31] This, of course, turned out to be true. Inspired by the anti-colonial struggle – many of the soldiers who revolted against the regime during the revolution had served in Portugal's African colonies – the revolution overturned the weakened regime in Portugal and brought an end to its colonial empire in Africa. The long guerrilla war had turned struggles in Guinea-Bissau, Mozambique and Angola into 'national liberation struggles which were consciously revolutionary', instead of mere independence movements.[32] The future looked promising and, as the Estado Novo military regime fell, anti-colonial activists in Portugal's African colonies rejoiced. But many who had participated in the liberation war, like Cruz, Cabral and Mondlane, weren't alive to see its end.

Mondlane, who insisted that his own thought and Frelimo's political project could not exist 'outside or above the Mozambican people itself', was killed by a bomb hidden in a book that was sent to his office in Dar es Salaam in 1969, at the height of the Mozambican war of independence. 'The assassination', writes Natalia Telepneva, 'had clear signs of Portuguese involvement, and evidence pointed to the so-called Aginter Press, a clandestine network of sleeper agents who fought against Portugal's enemies in Africa' (though the involvement of disgruntled Frelimo cadres was also likely).[33] Mondlane's death ignited a long leadership crisis, which was only resolved when Samora Machel assumed the presidency in 1970, with Santos as his vice president. But Machel would die in a mysterious plane crash in 1986.[34] Cabral was assassinated in 1973 – shortly before Guinea-Bissau and Cape Verde gained formal independence – in a last-ditch attempt by Portuguese fascism to hold on to its 'overseas territories'. The murder was carried out by disgruntled PAIGC cadres who opposed the dominance of Cape Verdeans in the national liberation movement. Andrade, who had rejected the MPLA's post-independence authoritarian turn, chose self-exile in Guinea-Bissau. Adding to these names those that were killed, exiled or disillusioned during the first wave of African socialism – Pio Pinto, Maryse Condé, Patrice Lumumba, A.M. Babu and Andrée Blouin – we begin to get a clearer sense of how violent and calculated efforts to suppress Red Africa have been.

The anti-colonial feminist Andrée Blouin, whose important work leading women's organisations and working with post-independence governments across the continent has yet to be fully recognised, offers a fascinating portrait of the hopes, failures and contradictions of national liberation. In *My Country, Africa: Autobiography of the Black Pasionaria* (1983), Blouin recounts her political career, beginning from her hometown Bangui (in what is today the Central African Republic) to Guinea, Madagascar and eventually the Democratic Republic of Congo, where she becomes a key figure in the cabinet of Patrice Lumumba.[35] (The subtitle of the book, 'Autobiography of the Black Pasionaria', alludes to the sexist and exoticised portrayals of Blouin, a revolutionary Black woman, in European and American media.) Blouin, who would have undoubtedly described herself as part of the national liberation tradition, chose a title for her autobiography that is critical of the limited and traditionally masculine view of the nation – that of identity as territory – which draws maps and establishes belonging. Blouin was often unable to impact as she wished the post-independence politics of the countries whose liberation she dedicated her life to. But she nonetheless insisted that they were not examples of *failed* decolonisation, but sites where a multiplicity of conceptions of decolonisation were articulated.

Blouin's was a truly revolutionary life. In her autobiography, she recounts her childhood through two interrelated narratives: first, her experiences in an orphanage for mixed-race girls in Brazzaville, and second, her relationship with her parents. Blouin explains that because children from mixed relationships epitomised the fallibility of white men and their weakness for Black women, she was never claimed by her father. Instead, she was sent to live and work in an orphanage. Blouin recalls the small cruelties that the girls at the orphanage were subjected to. The vivid descriptions of hunger, humiliation and what can only be described as torture are difficult to read. In a shocking passage, Blouin describes refusing to eat the rotten food served at the orphanage and choosing instead to eat the moist clay from the walls of her residence building. After weeks of this she falls ill and is taken to the hospital, and her desperate decision becomes a small act of rebellion. The nuns at the orphanage are only accountable to the colonial authorities, who think that they are doing charitable Christian work by running the mission. When the authorities come to inspect the orphanage, the nuns, embarrassed by its dismal condition, are forced to curb some of their worst excesses. But Blouin's rebellion does little to make the daily humiliation, religious indoctrination and labour exploitation – the girls are forced to sow and embroider to finance the orphanage – more bearable.[36]

Blouin's rebellions are also inspired by her mother, whose early marriage to a (colonising) white man structured her emotional, physical and material desires. At first, she struggles to understand why her mother, Josephine, insists on having as many personal luxuries and material comforts as possible, and is often annoyed by her mother's obsession with what 'the right husband' could provide for her or her daughter. Blouin brusquely dismisses such obsessions, as she laments Josephine's 'dreadful naiveté' and her lack of understanding about colonialism.[37] In their relationship, the roles of mother and daughter are sometimes reversed, and Blouin, who worries about her mother's fragility, is forced to take care of and protect her. But mother and daughter do share a common rejection of the oppressive structures that define their lives: the colonial authorities, the church and the family. While Blouin later stages her acts of rebellion in the political sphere of national liberation, Josephine engages in everyday rebellions that subvert the authority of her husband, the colonial system or village traditions so that she may live as she likes. Aren't these seemingly small acts of rebellion utterly impressive considering the systems of oppression Josephine is forced to endure?

Blouin concludes that although her mother's life was shaped by colonialism she never truly rejected it, choosing instead to submit and seek whatever freedom she could within the confines of colonial society. Nonetheless, Josephine's rebellion becomes an inspiration for Blouin's later, more confrontational anti-colonial activism. After moving to Guinea with her second husband, André,

Blouin becomes involved in the anti-colonial struggle. In 1957, she joins Sékou Touré's Rassemblement Démocratique Africain (RDA), which plays a key role in her political awakening (she calls Touré 'the catalyst of my political commitment').[38] The turning point in her life comes when Blouin is herself trying to balance the role of mother with a newfound role as an anti-colonial revolutionary. She describes, for example, leaving her daughter, 'very ill with toxicosis', at home in the care of her doctor because she is desperately needed at a political rally. Blouin has now made her choice: her life belongs to the African revolution. When André, who is employed by a French mining company, is let go (presumably due to Blouin's activism with the RDA), the family is forced to leave Guinea for Madagascar. But as soon as Guinea is granted its independence, they return to where Blouin's political life had begun.

Following a political meeting with Congolese anti-colonial nationalists in Conakry, Blouin is tasked with organising Congolese women as the head of the women's division of the African Solidarity Party, the main nationalist party in the Belgian Congo (today the DRC). She notices a growing awareness among the women of the need to liberate themselves not only from colonialism, but from customs like the dowry system – which, Blouin argues, treats women as 'mere chattel' of fathers and husbands – and the Catholic and Protestant missions that play a key part in colonial oppression by teaching 'ignorance, apathy and submission'.[39] She also begins to understand the crucial role that ordinary Congolese women played in the project of national liberation. She recounts the story of a woman named Augustine. Augustine works as a promoter for the Polar beer brand – Patrice Lumumba was also a former promoter – but is recruited by Blouin to use her influence and popularity among the people to promote the participation of women in the anti-colonial struggle. Such stories too rarely appear in official narratives about national liberation, and it's only thanks to Blouin's writing that we can gain insight into the crucial role that women like Augustine played in the history of national liberation in Africa.[40]

Blouin later becomes a key figure in the movement for Congolese independence and a close advisor to Lumumba, the DRC's first post-independence prime minister. Towards the end of her autobiography, she retraces the events leading up the climax of her political life: the Congo Crisis, particularly Lumumba's assassination in January 1961, which put an end to the hopes of national liberation in the country. Blouin is at the centre of the action as she attempts to bridge divides between different factions to help them work towards their common aims. But she quickly realises 'the betrayal of Africa has been the work of our brothers': Lumumba's rival, the pro-Western centrist Joseph Kasavubu, who is closely involved with the United States, flaunts the leftist Lumumba's mandate to form a government and attempts to form his own instead.[41] Blouin is sent to Rome to rally support for the Lumumba government, but is hounded by the Belgian authorities and escapes to Touré's Guinea. Unable to return to the DRC, Blouin is forced to listen to Lumumba's famous independence speech on 30 June 1960 from exile in Conakry. When Blouin eventually returns, after Lumumba has officially formed a government, she comes back to a country in crisis. And, as the US- and Belgian-backed general Mobutu appears on the scene, the undoing of the nationalist revolution seems certain.

This is, in some ways, a familiar narrative about the decline of national liberation. But what is interesting about Blouin's account of the Congo Crisis is how harshly she judges Lumumba, whom she often describes as too good-natured, timid and, at times, naive. Blouin's portrait of Lumumba makes him appear in a new light. She vividly describes the moment when Lumumba turns himself in after his wife is arrested – a dramatic moment not only for his family but for Black radicals all over the world. For Blouin, his inability to put the needs of the nation over those of his family, as she had often done, constitutes nothing short of the betrayal of national liberation. Blouin gives the strong impression that the African revolution, to borrow a phrase from Fanon, would have been more radical if the women responsible for igniting it had found a place in post-independence governments, or if they had been more intimately involved in the formal process of decolonisation. At the end of the book, Blouin writes, 'I only regret that I was not given the right, in my sex, to go as far as I could.'[42] What could Blouin have achieved if her gender hadn't held her back? Surely, the project of national liberation would have been more successful for it. As we labour to recover silenced histories of Black radicalism and leftist anti-colonial thought, we must always remember: Red Africa is hers, too.

Afterword

On the night of 20 October 2020, soldiers from the Nigerian army opened fire on unarmed protestors at the Lekki Toll Gate in Logos State. There were forty-eight casualties, including eleven people killed and four missing and presumed dead. The protestors had organised the demonstration as part of the #EndSars movement, which called for an end to police violence in Nigeria and the disbanding of the Special Anti-Robbery Squad (SARS), a unit notorious for its involvement in extrajudicial killings. #EndSars had originally been founded in 2017, following a peaceful protest by Nigerian activists who hoped to bring public awareness to the unit's violent and illegal actions. The movement went quiet for a few years, but in early October 2020 a viral video showing SARS officers brutalizing and robbing a young man revived the hashtag on social media. Nigerians from all over the country were soon expressing their frustration with the neo-colonial state, which routinely subjects its citizens to the repression of public freedoms and wanton violence. This time, however, it was on display for the world to see: witnesses live-streamed the shooting and shared images on social media.

The murders of Breonna Taylor and George Floyd in the United States earlier that year had brought media attention to the Black struggle against police violence. The 'George Floyd rebellion', as it soon came to be known, reached its peak with the immolation of the Third Precinct police station in Minneapolis, Minnesota – the city where Floyd had been killed. But it also reached across the Atlantic, inspiring solidarity protests in European cities. In Britain and France, for example, protestors inspired by the rebellion, and by RhodesMustFall, demolished or defaced monuments to colonialism and slavery. While each protest addressed its own country's specific history of racism and state violence, the participants stood in solidarity with Black people in the United States. Like Floyd or Taylor, they too had been treated as second-class citizens and deemed 'undesirable' by the state. And though the scale and intensity of militarised policing in Europe is nowhere near that in the United States, they too had been subjected to a violent and racist criminal justice system.

This sudden surge in public interest allowed activists in Nigeria to project their grievances onto the world stage (though they were often overshadowed by events in Europe and the US). The political vocabulary of activists in the United States was sometimes useful, but #EndSars activists had a different object of discontent. While the George Floyd rebellion directed its demands at an imperialist and systemically racist state, #EndSars confronted a neo-colonial state, whose politicians, judiciary, military and police were mostly Black, too. #EndSars, then, wasn't simply a peripheral event in a summer of Black discontent that took place in Europe and the United States, or a protest that picked up the slogans of police abolition first articulated in the global north. Rather, it was a national youth movement of various classes – the middle class, working class and the unemployed, for example – which expressed public anger and frustration with the Nigerian state and its elites.[1] Though SARS was eventually disbanded, the protestors' other grievances were ignored. And despite the overwhelming amount of evidence, the state continued to deny the army's role in the Lekki shooting.

Neither the George Floyd rebellion nor #EndSars, however, could engender lasting institutional change. But what stopped these mass uprisings – which were, by all accounts, some of the largest in their respective national histories – from transforming rebellion and protest into revolutionary struggle? The answer to this question is complex, multifaceted and far beyond the scope of this short book. Instead, I have tried to gesture towards theoretical fault lines – the retreat of Black radicalism and 'decolonising' into the academy; the overemphasis on a diaspora perspective in how we understand Blackness; or a lack of serious engagement with the politics of national liberation and its relationship to the state – which have impacted our ability to develop what Ruth Wilson Gilmore calls an 'organic praxis': the production of knowledge that can be practically applied by struggles like the rebellion or #EndSars.[2] This lack of organic scholarship, which could provide much-needed ideological and strategic guidance, keeps us from transforming negative demands into positive articulations of a concrete political vision. Without this vision, we risk letting our radical demands be transformed into the mere repetition of slogans.

Despite differences in their objective conditions of struggle, it was clear that the rebellion and #EndSars were somehow connected.[3] Yet activists didn't have a shared language, organisation or ideology to build crucial solidarities between these two struggles for freedom. What was missing, it seemed, were the kind of displays of solidarity that were characteristic of twentieth-century anti-imperialism. Today, Bandung-era institutions like the Organization of Solidarity with the People of Asia, Africa and Latin America (OSPAAAL), which gave racialised, exploited or oppressed people in the global north *and* south a shared language to confront imperialism in all its guises, are desperately missed. OSPAAAL's propaganda campaigns directly addressed the imperialist United States' failure to curb institutional racism and state violence against Black people. The organisation considered itself a key bridge between the struggle of Black people in the United States and anti-imperialist movements in the Third World. But Black activists in the United States, too, knew that Third Worldist solidarity was a political necessity. As Malcolm X told his audience at the Audubon Ballroom in New York after returning from trips to Africa and the Middle East, 'As long as we think . . . that we should get Mississippi straightened out before we worry about the Congo, you'll never get Mississippi straightened out'.[4]

Africa is ostensibly part of capitalism's periphery, but the extraction of surplus value from the continent is central to its functioning. In a sense, Africa is where 'the relationship between transnational extractive projects . . . and the transformations of contemporary global finance . . . has been the most perversely tested'.[5] While multinationals reap the lion's share of profits from extractive projects, neo-colonial elites don't walk away empty-handed: a cursory glance at the Panama and Pandora

Papers and the Swiss Secrets leaks gives us an idea of the startling amounts they stash in tax havens abroad. This surplus value fuels global financial markets. But without the super-exploitation of Africa's labour or the plunder of its deposits of copper, cobalt, coltan, bauxite, platinum, diamonds or gold, the world economy would come to a halt. Political or state violence, like that enacted on #EndSars protestors, has long been a hallmark of neo-colonial states, who have tried to keep this extractive cycle going.[6] As the continent again becomes the site of militarised power struggles in a 'new Cold War', we should remember that anti-colonial Marxists, too, grappled with the question of how to take democratic control of the continent's resources while developing a 'counter-extractivist' practice.[7]

Our political horizons have changed since the end of the Bandung era, leaving us with no option but to place their politics into 'a new problem-space'.[8] The dream of national liberation as envisioned by anti-colonial Marxists might indeed have faded, but the utopias they envisioned have not yet been exhausted. Ngũgĩ wa Thiong'o, the Kenyan novelist and playwright who coined the term 'decolonising the mind', was of course right to insist that embracing or recovering Indigenous languages was a crucial step in the process of decolonisation. But Ngũgĩ was also a militant activist-intellectual, whose engagement against Kenya's neo-colonial ruling elite led to his arrest, detention and, eventually, exile. Ngũgĩ's concept of decolonisation was closely connected to the struggle for self-determination, and throughout his life he has remained a Marxist. But why hold on to a politics that is supposedly 'outdated', as some have claimed? The aim, I argue, is to remind ourselves that there were, and still are, alternative paths to emancipation – paths that have since been forgotten, but that remain as radical and transformative as ever. It is up to us to build a communism for our times from the ruins of Red Africa.

London, 8 February 2023

Acknowledgements

I would first like to thank my editor, Rosie Warren, without whom this book would not exist. When we started speaking about my Salvage essay, I could never have imagined that this would be the outcome. Your encouragement has been invaluable throughout this process.

Thanks to China Miéville for his very considered edits on that original essay. And thanks to the Salvage Editorial Collective for never shying away from the big questions. The vision of building a communism of the ruins from 'Red Africa' owes a huge debt to the work that you all do. Let's continue to build it together.

I'd like to thank my production editor, Jeanne Tao, and my copy editor, Max Bach, for their patience as we transformed the manuscript into a book. And thanks to the entire Verso team for allowing me to write this book and for getting the word out. I know my work is in safe hands. I'm truly grateful.

Thank you also to the basis voor actuele kunst and the *London Review of Books* for first commissioning essays that found their way into this book. Special thanks to Alice Spawls for taking a chance on my writing and for giving me the space to truly research the subjects of my pieces for the *LRB*.

I'd also like to thank Anti-imperialists for Global Justice, especially Amanda Latimer and Andy Higginbottom, for sharing their experience, knowledge and advice. Your work as educators and activists continues to inspire a new generation of anti-imperialists. A big thank you to Manjeet Ramgotra, whose teaching first sparked my interest in political theory.

Thank you to Farhaana and Brekhna of Hajar Press for showing me that a different way of publishing is possible. And thanks to Gaz for sharing my vision of a new kind of publication. It's an uphill battle, but it's worth it. Thank you to all my former colleagues at Foyles bookshop in London. Though booksellers never get the credit they deserve, this work would be impossible without you.

This book has been shaped by countless conversations with more people than I could hope to name here. Jamie, Sharon, Oly and Hannah, thanks for all the long chats we had when this book was forming in my mind. Mattie, Tom and Leila, thanks for always helping me think from a different perspective. Thank you to Fakher and Josh for keeping me grounded. And a huge thank you to Ellie, whose unwavering support while I was writing this book kept me going.

Writing is a collective endeavour and there are, of course, many more people I'd like to thank. If we ever sat down somewhere to talk life, politics or anything else, you know who you are.

Lastly, I would like to thank my parents, Elke and Isaiah, for their continued encouragement and support. Without you, none of this would have been possible. I'm especially grateful for the invaluable advice and intellectual guidance of my sister, Christine. I'll never stop learning from you.

I'd like to dedicate this book to my grandparents, Philomina and Karl.

The author and publisher would like to express their gratitude to the following publications in which earlier versions of chapters of this book were first published. Chapters 3 and 7 include reworked materials originally published as 'Resistance from Elsewhere' (2022) and 'Poison Is Better' (2023) by the *London Review of Books*. Chapters 6 and 7 include reworked materials from 'The Horizon of National Liberation', originally published as part of the ExitStateCraft" series on *Prospections*, basis voor actuele kunst, Utrecht, 2021.

Notes

Preface

1 RhodesMustFall's message resonated with Black students in Europe and the United States, too. Soon, RMF chapters at Harvard and Oxford were challenging their own institutions about links to colonialism and slavery, or the lack of curriculum reform.

2 gamEdze, gamedZe; 'Anxiety, Afropessimism, and the University Shutdown', *South Atlantic Quarterly* 118:1, 1 January 2019, 215–25. See also Rahul Rao, 'Neoliberal Antiracism and the British University', *Radical Philosophy* 208, Autumn 2020, 47–54.

3 The terms 'African', 'Indian' and 'Coloured' have been placed in quotation marks to reflect that Biko rejected these colonial political identities.

4 'Hopeless Africa', *Economist*, 11 May 2000.

5 'The Heart of the Matter', *Economist*, 11 May 2000.

6 Peter Mwai, 'Are Military Takeovers on the Rise in Africa?', *BBC News,* 2 February 2022.

7 Greg Thomas, 'Afro-Blue Notes: The Death of Afro-pessimism (2.0)?', *Theory and Event* 21:1, 2018, 297.

8 Olúfẹ́mi Táíwò, *Against Decolonisation: Taking African Agency Seriously*, London: Hurst Publishers, 2022.

9 Tricontinental Institute for Social Research, 'Ten Theses on Marxism and National Liberation: Dossier 56', September 2022.

10 In 2016, the London-based Calvert 22 Foundation hosted the Red Africa seasonal programme, which explored 'the legacy of cultural relationships between Africa, the Soviet Union and related countries'

during the Cold War. My use of the phrase 'Red Africa' takes inspiration from this project, but hopes to extend it conceptually by foregrounding the agency of anti-colonial Marxists in Africa.

11 David Scott, *Conscripts of Modernity: The Tragedy of Colonial Enlightenment*, Durham, NC: Duke University Press, 2005, 1.

1. Decolonisation and the Decline of the 'Bandung Spirit'

1 Christopher J. Lee, introduction to *Making a World after Empire: The Bandung Moment and Its Political Afterlives*, ed. Christopher J. Lee, Athens: Ohio University Press, 2010, 10.

2 Vijay Prashad, *The Darker Nations: A People's History of the Third World*, New York: New Press, 2008, 34.

3 Richard Wright, *The Color Curtain: A Report on the Bandung Conference*, Jackson: University Press of Mississippi, 1995, 11–12.

4 Though only India, Burma (Myanmar) and Indonesia officially supported a position of nonalignment in 1955, it became an essential aspect of Third World solidarity in the following years.

5 While the nations assembled at Bandung shared a commitment to anti-colonial and anti-imperialist politics, they often held conflicting ideological positions and pursued different strategic objectives. Ceylon (now Sri Lanka) and Pakistan, for example, were pro-Western and anti-communist, whereas North Vietnam and China were officially communist states.

6 Tricontinental Institute for Social Research, 'Homage to OSPAAAL, the Organization of Solidarity for the Peoples of Asia, Africa, and Latin America: Newsletter Thirty-One', August 2019.

7 Leslie James, *George Padmore and Decolonization from Below: Pan-Africanism, the Cold War, and the End of Empire*, Basingstoke: Palgrave Macmillan, 2015, 16.

8 James, *Padmore and Decolonization from Below*, 178.

9 Conflicts between Bandung nations, such as the Sino-Indian border conflict or disputes between India and Pakistan, contributed to the decline of Third World solidarity. Moreover, some Third World nations were themselves engaged in colonial occupations of territories whose claims to sovereignty were made invisible by the Bandung project. As Quito Swan has pointed out, Indonesia used 'Bandung as a platform to solidify support from its African and Asian allies for its claims to West Papua' by framing

the occupation as a form of resistance to Dutch colonialism. See Quito Swann, 'Blinded by Bandung? Illuminating West Papua, Senegal, and the Black Pacific', *Radical History Review*, 131, 2018, 58–81, 60.

10 Prashad, *The Darker Nations*, 222.

11 Samir Amin, 'Democracy and National Strategy in the Periphery', *Third World Quarterly* 9:4, 1987, 1156.

12 Quinn Slobodian, *Globalists: The End of Empire and the Birth of Neoliberalism*, Cambridge, MA: Harvard University Press, 2018, 4, 15.

13 Ruth Wilson Gilmore, 'Public Enemies and Private Intellectuals: Apartheid USA', *Race and Class* 35:1, 1993, 78.

14 David Scott, *Conscripts of Modernity: The Tragedy of Colonial Enlightenment*, Durham, NC: Duke University Press, 2005, 210.

15 Hubert Harrison, 'Our International Consciousness', in *When Africa Awakes*, Baltimore: Black Classic Press, 1997, 100–1, 103.

16 Kevin Ochieng Okoth, 'Decolonisation and Its Discontents', *Salvage*, 22 September 2021.

17 Nelson Maldonado-Torres, 'Enrique Dussel's Liberation Thought in the Decolonial Turn', *Transmodernity: Journal of Peripheral Cultural Production of the Luso-Hispanic World* 1:1, 2011, 7.

18 Walter Mignolo and Catherine E. Walsh, *On Decoloniality: Concepts, Analytics, Praxis*, Durham, NC: Duke University Press, 2018, 139.

19 Olúfẹ́mi O. Táíwò, *Elite Capture: How the Powerful Took Over Identity Politics and Everything Else*, Chicago: Haymarket Books, 2022, 10.

20 Silvia Rivera Cusicanqui, '*Ch'ixinakax utxiwa*: A Reflection on the Practices and Discourses of Decolonization', *South Atlantic Quarterly* 111:1, 1 January 2012, 97.

21 Ibid., 104.

22 Mignolo and Walsh, *On Decoloniality*, 136.

23 Nelson Maldonado-Torres, 'On the Coloniality of Being', *Cultural Studies* 21:2–3, 2007, 243.

24 Mignolo and Walsh, *On Decoloniality*, 115.

25 Gilmore, 'Public Enemies and Private Intellectuals', 71.

26 Achille Mbembe, *Out of the Dark Night: Essays on Decolonization*, New York: Columbia University Press, 2021, 79.

27 Achille Mbembe, 'African Modes of Self-Writing', *Public Culture* 14:1, 1 January 2002, 241.

28 Mbembe, 'African Modes of Self-Writing', 242.

29 Ibid., 244.

30 Okoth, 'Decolonisation and Its Discontents'.

31 Adom Getachew, *Worldmaking after Empire: The Rise and Fall of Self-Determination*, Princeton, NJ: Princeton University Press, 2019, 181.

32 Ibid., 10.

33 Michael Hardt and Antonio Negri, *Empire*, vol. 1, Cambridge, MA: Harvard University Press, 2003, 132.

34 Erez Manela, *The Wilsonian Moment: Self-Determination and the International Origins of Anticolonial Nationalism*, Oxford: Oxford University Press, 2007, 40.

35 Ibid., 43.

36 For more on how the US didn't accept minority rights for its own internal minorities (i.e., Indigenous peoples), see Nick Estes, *Our History Is the Future: Standing Rock versus the Dakota Access Pipeline, and the Long Tradition of Indigenous Resistance*, London: Verso, 2019.

37 Getachew, *Worldmaking after Empire*, 10.

38 Alden Young, 'How to Think about Ethiopian Politics Today', *Africa Is a Country*, November 2020.

2. From Black Studies to Afro-pessimism

1 Stanley Crouch, introduction to *The Crisis of the Negro Intellectual: A Historical Analysis of the Failure of Black Leadership*, by Harold Cruse, New York: New York Review Books, 2005, 2.

2 Ibram X. Kendi, *The Black Campus Movement: Black Students and the Racial Reconstitution of Higher Education, 1965–1972*, New York: Palgrave Macmillan, 2012, xiii.

3 Brent H. Belvin, 'Malcolm X Liberation University: An Experiment in Independent Black Education', MA thesis, North Carolina State University, 6 October 2004, 70.

4 Otis Alexander, 'Institute of the Black World (1969–1983)', 9 October 2022, blackpast.org.

5 Derrick E. White, 'An Independent Approach to Black Studies: The Institute of the Black World (IBW) and Its Evaluation and Support of Black Studies', *Journal of African American Studies* 16, 2012, 80.

6 Ibid., 83.

7 Colleen Lye, 'US Ethnic Studies and Third Worldism, 40 Years Later', *Inter-Asia Cultural Studies* 11:2, 2010, 188.

8 One of the earliest protests at San Francisco State, for example, built on the anti-war movement, responding to the university's 'acquiescence to

an organization that collected data on potential draftees into the Vietnam War'. See Jay Caspian Kang, *The Loneliest Americans*, New York: Crown, 2021, 48.

9 Lisa Lowe, *Immigrant Acts: On Asian American Cultural Politics*, Durham, NC: Duke University Press, 1996, 27.

10 Lye, 'US Ethnic Studies and Third Worldism', 189.

11 Martha Biondi, *The Black Revolution on Campus*, Berkeley: University of California Press, 2012, 233, 206.

12 Ibid., 211–40.

13 Ruth Wilson Gilmore, 'Decorative Beasts: Dogging the Academy in the Late 20th Century', in *Abolition Geography: Essays Towards Liberation*, London: Verso, 2022.

14 Even Cruse, a stalwart of the Black left and former member of the Communist Party, was offered a permanent position in the Department of African American Studies at the University of Michigan.

15 Biondi, *Black Revolution on Campus*, 5.

16 Andrew J. Douglas and Jared Loggins, 'The Lost Promise of Black Study', *Boston Review*, 28 September 2021.

17 Jared Sexton, 'Ante-Anti-Blackness: Afterthoughts', *Lateral* 1:1 (May 2012).

18 Frank B. Wilderson III, *Incognegro: A Memoir of Exile and Apartheid*, Durham, NC: Duke University Press, 2015, 422.

19 Wilderson points to the 1993 murder of the African National Congress activist Chris Hani, leader of the South African Communist Party and chief of staff of uMkhonto we Sizwe (MK, the armed wing of the ANC) as the moment he decided to abandon Marxist-Leninist politics and turn towards AP 2.0. At the time, Wilderson was also a member of MK.

20 Greg Tate, 'Afropessimism and Its Discontents', *Nation*, 17 September 2021, thenation.com.

21 Adolph Reed Jr., 'Afropessimism, or Black Studies as a Class Project', 26 September 2022, nonsite.org.

22 Sexton, 'Ante-Anti-Blackness'.

23 Ontology, as it is defined in philosophy, denotes the branch of metaphysics dealing with the nature of being, not being itself. When Calvin Warren argues that the Black and ontology are incompatible, he is simply saying: 'The question of the meaning of Black being is unanswerable because we've lacked a philosophical tradition that would provide refuge and clarity'. The Black is thus condemned to a state of metaphysical homelessness because ontology cannot give them the tools to understand their own existence. See Calvin L. Warren, *Ontological Terror: Blackness, Nihilism, and Emancipation*, Durham, NC: Duke University Press, 2018, 59.

24 Frank B. Wilderson III, 'The Black Liberation Army and the Paradox of Political Engagement', in *Postcoloniality – Decoloniality – Black Critique: Joints and Fissures*, ed. Sabine Bröck-Sallah and Carsten Junker, Frankfurt: Campus Verlag, 2014, 183.

25 Frank B. Wilderson III, 'Blacks and the Master/Slave Relation', in *Afropessimism: An Introduction*, Minneapolis: Racked & Dispatched, 2017, 25.

26 Warren, *Ontological Terror*, 48.

27 Frank B. Wilderson III, *Afropessimism*, New York: Liveright, 2021, 16.

28 Ibid., 176.

29 Ibid., 216–19.

30 Jared Sexton, 'The Social Life of Social Death', in *Time, Temporality and Violence in International Relations: (De)fatalizing the Present, Forging Radical Alternatives*, ed. Anna M. Agathangelou and Kyle D. Killian, Abingdon: Routledge, 2016, 67.

31 Frank B. Wilderson III, ' "We're Trying to Destroy the World": Anti-Blackness and Police Violence after Ferguson', in *Shifting Corporealities in Contemporary Performance*, ed. Marina Gržinić and Aneta Stojnić, Cham: Springer International, 2018, 45–59.

32 Annie Olaloku-Teriba, 'Afro-pessimism and the (Un)logic of Anti-Blackness', *Historical Materialism*, 30 July 2018, historicalmaterialism .org.

33 Reed, 'Afropessimism, or Black Studies as a Class Project'.

34 As Saidiya Hartman has pointed out, 'Black suffering was quickly turned into white pedagogy'. The fastest-selling book at the time of the rebellion was the white 'diversity consultant' Robin DiAngelo's 2018 self-help anti-racism book *White Fragility*. See Saidiya Hartman, 'Saidiya Hartman on Insurgent Histories and the Abolitionist Imaginary', *Artforum*, 14 July 2020, artforum.com.

35 Tate, 'Afropessimism and Its Discontents'.

36 Saidiya Hartman, *Lose Your Mother: A Journey along the Atlantic Slave Route*, New York: Farrar, Straus & Giroux, 2008, 6.

37 Saidiya Hartman, *Scenes of Subjection: Terror, Slavery, and Self-Making in Nineteenth-Century America*, New York: Oxford University Press, 1997, 6.

38 Instead of focusing on the routinized displays of 'shocking and terrible' violence against enslaved people, Hartman narrows in on 'those scenes of terror which can hardly be discerned – slaves dancing in the quarters, the outrageous dark antics of the minstrel stage, the constitution of humanity in slave law, and the fashioning of the self-possessed individual'. Hartman, *Scenes of Subjection*, 4.

39 Saidiya Hartman, *Wayward Lives, Beautiful Experiments: Intimate Histories of Riotous Black Girls, Troublesome Women, and Queer Radicals*, London: Serpent's Tail, 2019, 227.

40 Ibid., 9.

41 Gloria Wekker, 'Afropessimism', *European Journal of Women's Studies* 28:1, February 2021, 86–97.

42 Ibid., 10.

43 Fred Moten and Stefano Harney, *All Incomplete*, Colchester: Minor Compositions, 2021, 74.

44 Ibid., 85.

45 Fred Moten and Stefano Harney, 'The University and the Undercommons', *Social Text* 22:2, 2004, 104.

46 Cedric J. Robinson and Erica R. Edwards, *The Terms of Order: Political Science and the Myth of Leadership*, Chapel Hill: University of North Carolina Press, 2016, 7.

47 Fred Moten, *The Universal Machine: Consent Not to Be a Single Being*, Durham, NC: Duke University Press, 2018, 234.

48 Olaloku-Teriba, 'Afro-pessimism and the (Un)logic of Anti-Blackness', 96–122.

49 Sexton, 'Ante-Anti-Blackness', 8.

50 This explains Moten's focus on improvisation in Black performance art as acts of fugitive political resistance.

51 Steve Martinot and Jared Sexton, 'The Avant-Garde of White Supremacy', *Social Identities* 9:2, June 2003, 178.

52 Frank B. Wilderson III, *Red, White and Black: Cinema and the Structure of U.S. Antagonisms*, Durham, NC: Duke University Press, 2010, 79.

53 The AP 2.0 dismissal and erasure of anti-colonial thought is even more bizarre when we consider Wilderson's biography. How did someone who was a member of the African National Congress's military wing, Umkhonto we Sizwe (MK), and a fierce left critic of Nelson Mandela create a theoretical apparatus that is incapable of dealing with the realities of imperialism and neo-colonialism on the African continent?

54 Martinot and Sexton, 'Avant-Garde of White Supremacy'.

55 Frank B. Wilderson III, 'Gramsci's Black Marx: Whither the Slave in Civil Society?', *Social Identities* 9:2, June 2003, 225–40.

56 Wilderson, *Afropessimism*, 223.

57 David Eltis and David Richardson, *Atlas of the Transatlantic Slave Trade*, New Haven, CT: Yale University Press, 2015.

58 While these discourses take issue with the effects of neoliberal reforms on the university, they ironically work to enable Black studies' flourishing within the academy. Their account of resistance refuses to

confront either the neoliberal university, multinational corporations or the state because, they argue, to do so would be to recognise the legitimacy of these institutions. The four authors discussed in this chapter are all employed by elite higher education institutions.

59 Hartman, for example, has argued that 'the Marxist narrative of modes of production . . . seemed inadequate when accounting for slavery'. See Elias Rodriques, 'How Saidiya Hartman Changed the Study of Black Life', *Nation*, 3 November 2022, thenation.com.

60 'If national liberation – as it moves through the discourse of self-determination – is a political problem', write Moten and Harney, 'then that is also the extent to which it ought not to be our problem, however much it gives us problems'. Moten and Harney, *All Incomplete*, 150.

3. Racial Capitalism and the Afterlives of Slavery

1 Robin D.G. Kelley, 'Why Black Marxism, Why Now?', *Boston Review*, 1 February 2021.

2 Cedric J. Robinson, *An Anthropology of Marxism*, London: Pluto Press, 2019, 6.

3 Amílcar Cabral and PAIGC, *Unity and Struggle: Speeches and Writings*, trans. Michael Wolfers, New York: Monthly Review Press, 2016, 124.

4 Ibid., 125.

5 Avery F. Gordon, preface to Robinson, *An Anthropology of Marxism*, xxvii.

6 Enzo Traverso, *Revolution: An Intellectual History*, London: Verso, 2021, 49.

7 Cedric J. Robinson, 'Slavery and the Platonic Origins of Anti-democracy', in *Cedric J. Robinson: On Racial Capitalism, Black Internationalism, and Cultures of Resistance*, ed. H.L.T. Quan, London: Pluto Press, 2019, 127–46.

8 Karl Marx, *Capital: A Critique of Political Economy*, vol. 1, trans. Ben Fowkes, London: Penguin in association with New Left Review, 1990 [1976], 915.

9 *Marx and Engels Collected Works*, vol. 38, 101, cited in Kevin B. Anderson, *Marx at the Margins: On Nationalism, Ethnicity, and Non-Western Societies*, Chicago: University of Chicago Press, 2016, 83.

10 Michael Walzer, 'A Note on Racial Capitalism', *Dissent*, 29 July 2020.

11 Arun Kundnani, 'What Is Racial Capitalism?', 23 October 2020, kundnani.org.

12 Martin Legassick and David Hemson, *Foreign Investment and the Reproduction of Racial Capitalism in South Africa*, London: Anti-Apartheid Movement, 1976.

13 Cedric J. Robinson, *Black Marxism: The Making of the Black Radical Tradition*, London: Penguin Classics, 2021, 9.

14 Cedric J. Robinson, 'White Signs in Black Times: The Politics of Representation in Dominant Texts', in *On Racial Capitalism*, 189.

15 Chris Chen, 'The Limit Point of Capitalist Equality', *Endnotes*, no. 3, 2013.

16 Stephanie Smallwood, 'What Slavery Tells Us about Marx', *Boston Review*, 21 February 2018. Italics in original.

17 Andrew Higginbottom, 'Enslaved African Labour: Violent Racial Capitalism', in *The Palgrave Encyclopedia of Imperialism and Anti-Imperialism*, ed. Immanuel Ness and Zak Cope, Cham: Springer International, 2021, 736–51.

18 Nikhil Pal Singh, 'On Race, Violence, and So-Called Primitive Accumulation', *Social Text* 34:3, 2016, 128.

19 For more on this, see Robin Blackburn's *The Overthrow of Colonial Slavery, 1776–1848*, London: Verso, 1988; *The Making of New World Slavery: From the Baroque to the Modern, 1492–1800*, London: Verso, 2010; and *The American Crucible: Slavery, Emancipation and Human Rights*, London: Verso, 2013.

20 Blackburn, *Overthrow of Colonial Slavery*, 7.

21 Ibid., 8.

22 Mintz, quoted in David Scott, 'Modernity That Predated the Modern: Sidney Mintz's Caribbean', *History Workshop Journal* 58, 2004, 191. Italics in original.

23 As Amanda Latimer explains: 'Superexploitation manifests in a variety of low-wage, physically exhausting, and often dangerous work. It involves the extraction of an "extra" degree of surplus value from expended labor power, which manifests as the lowering of wages below the level necessary for the worker to reproduce their labor power.' It is often structurally linked to other forms of oppression which facilitate a more extreme form of exploitation. For more on this, see Amanda Latimer, 'Super-Exploitation, the Race to the Bottom, and the Missing International', in *The Palgrave Encyclopedia of Imperialism and Anti-Imperialism*, 2546.

24 Blackburn, *Overthrow of Colonial Slavery*, 535. As Higginbottom explains, 'What is missing between two senses of mode of production presented as the universal and the particular is the intermediate concept of mode of exploitation, a concept present embryonically in

Marx in his contrast of the slavery of antiquity with modern capitalism.' Higginbottom, 'Enslaved African Labour', 748.

25 Blackburn, *Overthrow of Colonial Slavery*, 21.

26 Higginbottom, 'Enslaved African Labour', 749.

27 Greg Thomas, 'Afro-Blue Notes: The Death of Afro-pessimism (2.0)?', *Theory and Event*, 21:1, 2018, 297.

28 Walter Rodney, 'Plantation Society in Guyana', *Review* 4:4, 1981, 662.

29 Blackburn, *Overthrow of Colonial Slavery*, 11.

30 Eric Williams, *Capitalism and Slavery*, 3rd ed., Chapel Hill: University of North Carolina Press, 2021, 4.

31 Gerald Horne, 'The Politician-Scholar', *Nation*, 5 October 2021.

32 Blackburn, *Overthrow of Colonial Slavery*, 13.

33 In his PhD dissertation, Williams names possible reasons for this decline in profitability. First, British planters faced economic pressures due to foreign competition, which resulted in a collapse of sugar prices. Second, the liberalisation of trade with other plantation economies allowed the British to abolish slavery while continuing to benefit from enslaved labour. Third, the sugar economy had become less important for the British economy, owing to the expansion of the domestic industrial sector. See Eric E. Williams and D.W. Tomich, *The Economic Aspect of the Abolition of the West Indian Slave Trade and Slavery*, London: Rowman & Littlefield, 2014.

34 Williams didn't pay much attention to how the profits that were transferred to Europe and enabled industrialisation were made in the first place. For a more thorough analysis of the relationship between exploitation and unequal exchange, see Latimer, 'Super-Exploitation, the Race to the Bottom'.

35 Blackburn, *The American Crucible*, 307.

36 'Plantocracy' refers to a society where planters form the dominant class.

37 Blackburn, *Overthrow of Colonial Slavery*, 520.

38 Ibid., 529.

39 Sudhir Hazareesingh, *Black Spartacus: The Epic Life of Toussaint Louverture*, New York: Farrar, Straus and Giroux, 2020, 5.

40 Johnhenry Gonzalez, *Maroon Nation: A History of Revolutionary Haiti*, New Haven, CT: Yale University Press, 2019, 50.

41 Hazareesingh, *Black Spartacus*, 5.

42 Blackburn, *Overthrow of Colonial Slavery*, 259.

43 Gonzalez, *Maroon Nation*, 3.

44 Ibid., 38.

45 Rodney, 'Plantation Society in Guyana', 653.

46 Sidney W. Mintz, *Caribbean Transformations*, New York: Columbia University Press, 1989, 248.

47 Blackburn, *Overthrow of Colonial Slavery*, 528.

48 John Keene, *Counternarratives*, New York: New Directions, 2015.

49 Stella Dadzie, *A Kick in the Belly: Women, Slavery and Resistance*, London: Verso, 2021, 114.

50 Ibid., 123.

51 Adiele Eberechukwu Afigbo, *The Abolition of the Slave Trade in Southeastern Nigeria, 1885–1950*, Rochester, NY: University of Rochester Press, 2006.

52 Adaobi Tricia Nwaubani, 'The Descendants of Slaves in Nigeria Fight for Equality', *New Yorker*, 11 July 2019.

53 Moulaye Hassane, 'Ajami in Africa: The Use of Arabic Script in the Transcription of African Languages', in *The Meanings of Timbuktu*, ed. Shamil Jeppie and Bachir Diagne, Cape Town: HSRC Press in association with CODESRIA, 2008, 100.

54 Rahmane Idrissa, 'Mapping the Sahel', *New Left Review*, 132, 2021, 11.

55 Domenico Losurdo and Gregory Elliott, *Liberalism: A Counter-History*, London: Verso, 2014, 249.

56 Alexandre Popović, *The Revolt of African Slaves in Iraq in the 3rd/9th Century*, Princeton, NJ: M. Wiener; 1998, 3.

57 While there is some debate over the exact composition of the Zanj Rebellion, it is likely that peasants and Bedouins joined the revolting enslaved Africans.

58 Higginbottom, 'Enslaved African Labour', 736.

59 Blackburn, *Overthrow of Colonial Slavery*, 18.

60 Ibid., 525.

61 Losurdo and Elliott, *Liberalism*, 249.

62 Denise Ferreira da Silva, 'Facts of Blackness: Brazil Is Not Quite the United States . . . and Racial Politics in Brazil?', *Social Identities* 4:2, March 1998, 230.

63 Denise Ferreira da Silva, *Toward a Global Idea of Race*, Minneapolis: University of Minnesota Press, 2007, xxxvi.

4. Négritude and the (Mal)practice of Diaspora

1 Franklin Rosemont and Robin D.G. Kelley, eds., *Black, Brown, and Beige: Surrealist Writings from Africa and the Diaspora*, Austin: University of Texas Press, 2009.

2 Jean-Paul Sartre, 'Black Orpheus', trans. John MacCombie, *Massachusetts Review* 6:1, 1965, 18.

3 Souleymane Bachir Diagne, 'Négritude', *Stanford Encyclopedia of Philosophy*, 23 May 2018, plato.stanford.edu.

4 Souleymane Bachir Diagne argues that Senghor's statement 'Emotion is Negro, as reason is Hellenic' can be read as: 'Emotion is to African works of art what reason is to Hellenic statuary.' He takes Senghor's Négritude not as an ontology or epistemology, but simply as a comment on the contrasts between the aesthetics of the Hellenic tradition and African sculpture. This is a very charitable reading. See Souleymane Bachir Diagne, *African Art as Philosophy: Senghor, Bergson, and the Idea of Negritude*, trans. Chike Jeffers, London: Seagull Books, 2011, 71.

5 Césaire cited in ibid., 34. *Discours sur la Négritude* (A lecture on Négritude), from which this passage is quoted, was originally a lecture given on 26 February 1987 at Florida International University in Miami.

6 Suzanne Césaire, 'Surrealism and Us', in *The Great Camouflage: Writings of Dissent, 1941–1945*, ed. Daniel Maximin, trans. Keith L. Walker, Middletown, CT: Wesleyan University Press, 2012, 37–8.

7 Perry Anderson, *Considerations on Western Marxism*, London: Verso, 1987.

8 Léon-Gontran Damas, *Poètes d'expression française: D'Afrique Noire, Madagascar, Réunion, Guadeloupe, Martinique, Indochine, Guyane, 1900–1945* [French-language poets from black Africa, Madagascar, Réunion, Guadaloupe, Martinique, Indochina, Guyana, 1900–1945], Paris: Éditions du Seuil, 1947, 13.

9 Jared Sexton, 'Ante-Anti-Blackness: Afterthoughts', *Lateral* 1:1, May 2012.

10 Ali A. Mazrui, 'Black Orientalism? Further Reflections on "Wonders of the African World"', *Black Scholar* 30:1, 2000, 15–18.

11 Aimé Césaire, *Discourse on Colonialism*, trans. Joan Pinkham, New York: Monthly Review Press, 2000, 65–74.

12 Ibid., 14.

13 Gayatri Chakravorty Spivak, 'Subaltern Studies: Deconstructing Historiography', in *The Spivak Reader: Selected Works of Gayatri Chakravorty Spivak*, ed. Donna Landry and Gerald MacLean, New York: Routledge, 1996, 204.

14 Diagne, 'Négritude'.

15 Pascal Bianchini, 'The 1968 Years: Revolutionary Politics in Senegal', *Review of African Political Economy* 46:160, 3 April 2019, 184–203.

16 Florian Bobin, 'Omar Blondin Diop: Seeking Revolution in Senegal', *Review of African Political Economy*, 18 March 2020.

17 Diop was a Marxist anti-colonial activist who was active in both France and Senegal. He was arrested while plotting a guerrilla war against the Senghor government. Diop had received military training from the Palestinian Liberation Organization in Syria and the Black Panthers in Algeria.

18 Brent Hayes Edwards, *The Practice of Diaspora: Literature, Translation, and the Rise of Black Internationalism*, Cambridge, MA: Harvard University Press, 2003, 3.

19 Ibid., 6.

20 Edwards, *The Practice of Diaspora*, 12.

21 Jennifer Boittin, 'The Militant Black Men of Marseille and Paris, 1927–1937', in *Black France/France Noire*, ed. Trica Danielle Keaton, T. Denean Sharpley-Whiting and Tyler Stovall, Durham, NC: Duke University Press, 2012, 223.

22 Ibid., 230.

23 This also meant that Black workers were more open to organising alongside non-Black workers: while the LDRN's Paris branch only allowed Black men and their wives to attend meetings, the Marseille branch let non-Black men and women join.

24 Hakim Adi, *Pan-Africanism: A History*, London: Bloomsbury Academic, 2018, 96.

25 *Mestiço* was the Portuguese colonial codification for biracial or multiracial colonial subjects; *assimilado* refers to a social class of assimilated colonial subjects who were either *mestiço*, Black African or Afro-Portuguese.

26 In its internal report, the Soviet Writers' Union branded Diop a 'hostile bourgeois nationalist'.

27 Natalia Telepneva, *Cold War Liberation: The Soviet Union and the Collapse of the Portuguese Empire in Africa, 1961–1975*, Chapel Hill: University of North Carolina Press, 2021, 45.

28 Christopher Leigh Connery, 'The World Sixties', in *The Worlding Project: Doing Cultural Studies in the Era of Globalization*, ed. Rob Wilson and Christopher Leigh Connery, Berkeley, CA: North Atlantic Books, 2007, 77–108.

29 Amílcar Cabral, *Return to the Source: Selected Speeches*, New York: Monthly Review Press, 1973/74.

5. Whose Fanon? On Blackness and National Liberation

1 In *Whither Fanon* (2018), David Marriott offers a more nuanced portrait of Fanon which attempts to read his psychoanalytic texts alongside his political writing, taking as its starting premise the primacy of Fanon's clinical work. Though Marriott's account is impressive in scope, it does have some limitations. For example, Marriott switches back and forth between the Black and the colonised subject, using the latter to establish a theory of Blackness as '*n'est pas*', which he defines as an interruption of meaning. But this theoretical move erases the multiplicity of experiences of racialised colonial subjects, many of whom were not Black. See David S. Marriott, *Whither Fanon? Studies in the Blackness of Being*, Stanford, CA: Stanford University Press, 2018.

2 Frantz Fanon, *Black Skin, White Masks*, trans. Richard Philcox, New York: Grove Press, 2008, 91.

3 Frantz Fanon, *Alienation and Freedom*, trans. Steven Corcoran, ed. Jean Khalfa and Robert J.C. Young, London: Bloomsbury Academic, 2018, 32.

4 Ibid., 38.

5 Fanon, *Black Skin, White Masks*, 7.

6 Frantz Fanon, *The Wretched of the Earth*, trans. Constance Farrington, London: Penguin, 2001, 173–4.

7 Fanon, *Alienation and Freedom*, 17.

8 A.T. Judy, quoted in Lewis R. Gordon, *What Fanon Said: A Philosophical Introduction to His Life and Thought*, London: Hurst, 2015, 47.

9 As Sylvia Wynter puts it, the mode of subjectivity engendered in racialised people is a product of 'the contemporary West's genre-specific mode of sociogeny': they experience themselves 'in terms of the White masks, that were phenotypically normal only for the specific subset hereditary variation of the human species that are Europeans'. See Sylvia Wynter, 'Human Being as Noun? Or *Being Human* as Praxis? Towards the Autopoetic Turn/Overturn: A Manifesto', unpublished paper, posted on *The Frantz Fanon Blog*, 27 October 2014, readingfanon.blogspot.com.

10 Cedric J. Robinson, 'The Appropriation of Frantz Fanon', in *Cedric J. Robinson: On Racial Capitalism, Black Internationalism, and Cultures of Resistance*, ed. H.L.T. Quan, London: Pluto Press, 2019, 295.

11 Gordon, *What Fanon Said*, 18.

12 Fanon, *Wretched of the Earth*, 36.

13 Frantz Fanon, *A Dying Colonialism*, trans. Haakon Chevalier, New York: Grove Press, 2007, 179.

14 Gordon, *What Fanon Said*, 22.

15 Here, Fanon introduces the concept of 'living death' that is so central to Wilderson's, Jared Sexton's and Calvin Warren's work: 'He will feel empty, lifeless, in bodily struggle with death, a death on this side of death, a death in life'. But this is a condition that's not peculiar to the Black/Slave – the colonised Algerian also experiences the same chasm between their individual experience and the social structure. See Gordon, *What Fanon Said*, 77.

16 William Gardner Smith, *The Stone Face*, New York: New York Review Books, 2021.

17 Claude McKay, *The Negro in America,* trans. Robert Winter, ed. Alan McLeod, Port Washington, NY: Kennikat Press, 1979, 49; Smith, *The Stone Face*, xvii.

18 Adam Shatz, introduction to Smith, *The Stone Face*, xx.

19 Ibid., xxi.

20 Fanon, 'Colonial Wars and Mental Disorders', chap. 5 of *Wretched of the Earth*.

21 Fanon often found himself at odds with the political demands of the Algerian struggle, too – especially concerning the role of religion and culture in the anti-colonial movement. Despite his critical attitude towards European modernity, he remained, in many eyes, an *assimilé*, whose framework for understanding the Algerian situation was conditioned by his class position. See Anwār Omeish, 'Reading Fanon in Algeria, Reading Algeria beyond Fanon', *Africa Is a Country*, 11 January 2023, africasacountry.com.

22 '*The Wretched of the Earth* is prophetic, but not for the reasons Fanon would have wished. For all that he meant his book to be a manifesto for the coming revolution, he was aware of the potential pitfalls of decolonisation.' See Adam Shatz, 'Where Life Is Seized', *London Review of Books*, 19 January 2017, lrb.co.uk. Samir Amin, who describes the nationalist regime that emerged after independence as 'in no way more promising than Nasserism', is equally sober in his assessment of the achievements of the FLN.

6. Neo-colonialism, or, The Emptiness of Bearing One's Flag

1 Cheswayo Mphanza, *The Rinehart Frames*, Lincoln: University of Nebraska Press, 2021, 67–9.

2 Kwame Nkrumah, *Neo-Colonialism: The Last Stage of Imperialism*, New York: International Publishers, 1976, x.

3 Ayi Kwei Armah, *The Beautyful Ones Are Not Yet Born*, London: Heinemann, 2009, 126.

4 Mahmood Mamdani, *Neither Settler nor Native: The Making and Unmaking of Permanent Minorities*, Cambridge, MA: Belknap Press of Harvard University Press, 2020; Michael Neocosmos, *Thinking Freedom in Africa: Toward a Theory of Emancipatory Politics*, Johannesburg: Wits University Press, 2016.

5 Ernest Wamba dia Wamba, 'Experiences of Democracy in Africa: Reflections on Practices of Communalist Palaver as a Method of Resolving Contradictions', *New Frame*, 9 May 2019.

6 John S. Saul, 'The African Hero in Mozambican History: On Assassinations and Executions – Part I', *Review of African Political Economy* 47:163, 2 January 2020, 155.

7 Carl Gustav Rosberg and Thomas M. Callaghy, eds., *Socialism in Sub-Saharan Africa: A New Assessment*, Berkeley: Institute of International Studies, University of California, 1979, 1.

8 Robin D.G. Kelley, introduction to *Discourse on Colonialism*, by Aimé Césaire, New York: Monthly Review Press, 2000, 21.

9 W.O. Maloba, *The Anatomy of Neo-colonialism in Kenya: British Imperialism and Kenyatta, 1963–1978*, London: Palgrave Macmillan, 2018, 36.

10 Shiraz Durrani, ed., *Pio Gama Pinto: Kenya's Unsung Martyr, 1927–1965*, Nairobi: Vita Books, 2018, 57.

11 Maloba, *Neo-colonialism in Kenya*, 82–3.

12 Ibid., 21.

13 Pinto wrote: 'Kenya's Uhuru [freedom] must not be transformed into freedom to exploit, or freedom to be hungry, and live in ignorance. Uhuru must be Uhuru for the masses – Uhuru from exploitation, from ignorance, disease and poverty. The fighters must be honoured by the effective implementation of KANU's policy – a democratic, African, socialist state in which the people have the rights, in the words of the KANU election manifesto "to be free from economic exploitation and social inequality".' Pio Gama Pinto, 'Glimpses of Kenya's Nationalist Struggle', in Durrani, *Pio Gama Pinto*, 35.

14 Ibid., 102.

15 During the Nyerere presidency, Tanzania hosted exiled anti-colonial activists from across southern Africa, including the African National Congress (ANC) and Pan African Congress (PAC) from South Africa, the People's Movement for the Liberation of Angola (MPLA), the Mozambique Liberation Front (FRELIMO), the Zimbabwean African National Union (ZANU), the Zimbabwe African People's Union (ZAPU) and the South West Africa People's Organization (SWAPO) from Namibia.

16 They feared that the revolution would lead to a wave of leftist radicalization in East Africa, and that newly independent nations would align themselves with the Soviet Union. By supporting the US and the British, Nyerere showed that his Cold War politics were far from neutral.

17 Amrit Wilson, *The Threat of Liberation: Imperialism and Revolution in Zanzibar*, London: Pluto Press, 2013, 73.

18 Leo Zeilig, 'The Dar es Salaam Years', *Africa Is a Country*, 5 February 2022, africasacountry.com.

19 Walter Rodney, 'Tanzanian *Ujamaa* and Scientific Socialism', *African Review* 1:4, 1972, available at marxists.org.

20 Walter Rodney, 'Class Contradictions in Tanzania', in *The State in Tanzania: A Selection of Articles*, ed. Haroub Othman, Dar es Salaam: Dar es Salaam University Press, 1980, available at marxists .org.

21 Kwame Nkrumah, opening speech, in *Positive Action Conference for Peace and Security in Africa, Accra, 7th to 10th April, 1960*, Accra: Public Records and Archives Administration Department, 1960, PDF available at commons.wikimedia.org.

22 Kwame Nkrumah, *Revolutionary Path*, London: Panaf Books, 1973, 438.

23 Kwame Nkrumah, *Class Struggle in Africa*, London: Panaf Books, 1970, 27.

24 Paulin J. Hountondji, *The Struggle for Meaning: Reflections on Philosophy, Culture, and Democracy in Africa*, Athens: Ohio University Center for International Studies, 2002, 133.

25 Maryse Condé, *What Is Africa to Me? Fragments of a True-to-Life Autobiography*, trans. Richard Philcox, London: Seagull Books, 2017, 5.

26 She also learns about Félix Houphouët-Boigny, the politically moderate (read: anti-communist) and francophile (read: neo-colonial) leader of the Rassemblement Démocratique Africain (RDA). Houpheuët-Boigny – who is, of course, famous for maintaining a close partnership with Charles de Gaulle and Georges Pompidou, assisting the plotters of the coup that ousted Nkrumah, being involved in the coup that killed Thomas Sankara and working with US-backed anti-communist rebels in Angola – becomes the first disappointing political leader Condé encounters in West Africa.

27 Condé, *What Is Africa to Me?*, 105.

28 Ibid., 247.

7. Remnants of Red Africa

1 Among these self-described Marxist–Leninist movements, the short-lived but remarkably successful socialist project of Thomas Sankara in Burkina Faso stands out (1983–87). Sankara instituted a set of reforms, based on the values of self-sufficiency and mass mobilisation, which vastly improved living standards in the country. He was assassinated in 1987, following a military coup led by Blaise Compaoré, who reversed most of Sankara's anti-imperialist policies.

2 Maryse Condé, *What Is Africa to Me? Fragments of a True-to-Life Autobiography*, trans. Richard Philcox, New York: Seagull Books, 2017, 81.

3 Eduardo Mondlane explains class composition among the Portuguese settlers in Mozambique in an illuminating passage: '[The white colonial population in Portugal] is rather different from comparable small white minorities elsewhere in Africa in that, although members of it monopolise nearly all the important jobs in business and the professions, a large part of it is engaged in fairly menial pursuits: there are white artisans, white small-scale farmers, even white labourers. The reason for this is to be found in the low level of education and the widespread poverty in Portugal itself. Many of the immigrants to the colonies were poor peasants in Portugal; 50 per cent of immigrants are illiterate, and an even higher proportion unskilled.' Eduardo Mondlane, *The Struggle for Mozambique*. London: Zed Press, 1983, 56.

4 There was little incentive to pay African workers a living wage since the super-profits made by compensating them below the value of their labour power enabled white workers to receive higher wages.

5 See Branwen Gruffydd Jones, 'Anti-Racism and Emancipation in the Thought and Practice of Cabral, Neto, Mondlane and Machel', in *International Relations and Non-Western Thought*, ed. Robbie Shilliam, Abingdon: Routledge, 2011.

6 See Eduardo Mondlane, 'The Kitwe Papers: Race Relations and Portuguese Colonial Policy, with Special Reference to Mozambique', *Africa Today* 15:1, 1968.

7 Mondlane, *The Struggle for Mozambique*, 40.

8 There were many different legal codifications for forced or unfree African labour in colonial Mozambique; among these were correctional labour (instead of prison sentences), obligatory labour (six months of work for the state, a company or an individual), contract labour (under contract; failure to comply could lead to criminal charges), voluntary labour (mostly domestic work), forced cultivation (worker paid not for labour but for the product) and export

labour (workers sent abroad, mainly to South Africa, in return for payments to the Portuguese government). See ibid., 91.

9 Walter Rodney, 'Portuguese Attempts at Monopoly on the Upper Guinea Coast, 1580–1650', *Journal of African History* 6:3, 1965, 320

10 Mario Pinto de Andrade, 'Biographical Notes', in *Unity and Struggle: Speeches and Writings*, by Amílcar Cabral, ed. PAIGC, trans. Michael Wolfers, New York: Monthly Review, 2016, xxviii.

11 There were, of course, several attempts by PIDE to deprive the PAIGC of 'its most secure rear base by direct aggression against the Republic if Guinea'. Ibid., xxxiii.

12 Antonio Tomas, *Amílcar Cabral: The Life of a Reluctant Nationalist*, London: C. Hurst, 2019, 147.

13 Aquino de Bragança and Jacques Depelchin, 'From the Idealization of FRELIMO to the Understanding of the Recent History of Mozambique', *African Journal of Political Economy* 1:1, 1986.

14 Mondlane, *The Struggle for Mozambique*, 183.

15 Can we really claim, as Mahmood Mamdani does, that it is an 'unreasonable presumption' to argue that a 'new political community is constituted in the course of anti-colonial resistance'? Mahmood Mamdani, *Neither Settler nor Native: The Making and Unmaking of Permanent Minorities*, Cambridge, MA: Belknap Press of Harvard University Press, 2020, 34.

16 Tomas, *Amílcar Cabral*, 138.

17 Ibid., 142.

18 Ibid., 127.

19 Ibid., 12.

20 Natalia Telepneva, *Cold War Liberation: The Soviet Union and the Collapse of the Portuguese Empire in Africa, 1961–1975*, Chapel Hill: University of North Carolina Press, 2021, 95.

21 See Tom Meisenhelder, 'Amílcar Cabral's Theory of Class Suicide and Revolutionary Socialism', *Monthly Review* 45:6, 1993.

22 The idea that the petit bourgeoisie would abdicate their class position may seem naive to us now. At the time, however, the identification of the national petit bourgeoisie with the masses was a realistic prospect. As Jean-Paul Sartre argues in his introduction to Patrice Lumumba's collected speeches, the possible radicalisation of Lumumba – who prior to the struggle had held a petit bourgeois class position – by the masses and his identification with those masses was a serious concern for both Belgian and US intelligence. See Jean-Paul Sartre, introduction to *Lumumba Speaks: The Speeches and Writings of Patrice Lumumba, 1958–1961*, ed. Jean Van Lierde, trans. Helen R. Lane, Boston: Little, Brown, 1972, 49.

23 Amílcar Cabral, *Unity and Struggle: Speeches and Writings*, New York: Monthly Review Press, 2016, 128.

24 Ibid., 133.

25 These relationships came at a cost. Shortly after taking over Frelimo, Mondlane unknowingly let an American CIA agent named Leo Clinton Aldridge (alias Leo Milas) infiltrate the organisation. When Milas was exposed, Mondlane ousted him from the party and banned him from Dar es Salaam, where the exiled Frelimo leadership had set up its headquarters.

26 Some cadres pointed to Mondlane's reputation in the West as a skilled diplomat to argue that he was linked to the CIA. Despite the success of the ongoing war, he was never able to shed such suspicions.

27 Susan Williams, *White Malice: The CIA and the Neocolonisation of Africa*, London: C. Hurst, 2021.

28 George Roberts, 'The Assassination of Eduardo Mondlane: FRELIMO, Tanzania, and the Politics of Exile in Dar Es Salaam', *Cold War History* 17:1, 2 January 2017, 11.

29 Natalia Telepneva, ' "Code Name SEKRETÁŘ": Amílcar Cabral, Czechoslovakia and the Role of Human Intelligence during the Cold War', *International History Review*, 42:6, 2020, 3.

30 Ibid., 8.

31 Perry Anderson, 'Portugal and the End of Ultra-Colonialism (Part 3)', *New Left Review* 1:17, Winter 1962, 108.

32 Cedric J. Robinson, 'Amilcar Cabral and the Dialectic of Portuguese Colonialism', in *Cedric J. Robinson: On Racial Capitalism, Black Internationalism, and Cultures of Resistance*, ed. H.L.T. Quan, London: Pluto Press, 2019, 203.

33 Telepneva, *Cold War Liberation*, 132.

34 There were clear signs that apartheid South Africa was involved in Machel's death.

35 Andrée Blouin, *My Country, Africa: Autobiography of the Black Pasionaria*, trans. Jean MacKellar, New York: Praeger Publishers, 1983.

36 Ibid., 206.

37 Ibid., 178.

38 Ibid., 183.

39 Ibid., 208.

40 Ibid., 206.

41 Ibid., 238.

42 Ibid., 278.

Afterword

1 Nigeria has long been an archetypal neo-colony, with an economy characterised by extractive capitalism and the massive outflow of surplus value in the form of corporate profits abroad. Multinational companies like the fossil fuel giant Shell exploit the country's oil reserves and pollute its coastline, while local communities are often left with nothing (though Shell has recently been ordered to pay a US$15.9 million settlement to communities affected by an oil spill in the Niger Delta). In short, it is an oil-rich country whose population is poor. And while local elites, like Africa's richest man, Aliko Dangote (whose estimated net worth, according to *Forbes*, is around US$14.1 billion), profit handsomely from this arrangement, forty per cent of Nigerians live in absolute poverty.

2 Ruth Wilson Gilmore, 'Public Enemies and Private Intellectuals: Apartheid USA', *Race and Class*, 35:1, 1993, 73.

3 Tobi Haslett, 'Magic Actions: Looking Back on the George Floyd Rebellion', *n+1* 40, Summer 2021, nplusonemag.com.

4 Tariq Ali, 'Leaving Shabazz', *New Left Review* 69, May/June 2011, 159.

5 Achille Mbembe, *Out of the Dark Night: Essays on Decolonization*, New York: Columbia University Press, 2021, 36.

6 Daniel Selwyn, *Martial Mining*, London: London Mining Network, 2020.

7 Filipa César, 'Meteorisations: Reading Amílcar Cabral's Agronomy of Liberation', *Third Text* 32:2–3, 2018, 272.

8 David Scott, *Conscripts of Modernity: The Tragedy of Colonial Enlightenment*, Durham, NC: Duke University Press, 2005, 210.

Further Reading

1. Decolonisation and the Decline of the 'Bandung Spirit'

Prashad, Vijay. *The Darker Nations: A People's History of the Third World*. Paperback ed. A New Press People's History. New York: New Press, 2008.

Scott, David. *Conscripts of Modernity: The Tragedy of Colonial Enlightenment*. Durham, NC: Duke University Press, 2005.

Getachew, Adom. *Worldmaking after Empire: The Rise and Fall of Self-Determination*. Princeton, NJ: Princeton University Press, 2019.

Manela, Erez. *The Wilsonian Moment: Self-Determination and the International Origins of Anticolonial Nationalism*. Oxford: Oxford University Press, 2007.

Gilmore, Ruth Wilson. *Abolition Geography: Essays Towards Liberation*. Edited by Brenna Bhandar and Alberto Toscano. London: Verso, 2022.

Táíwò, Olúfẹ́mi. *Against Decolonisation: Taking African Agency Seriously*. London: Hurst & Company, 2022.

Cusicanqui, Silvia Rivera. '*Ch'ixinakax utxiwa*: A Reflection on the Practices and Discourses of Decolonization'. *South Atlantic Quarterly*, 111:1, 1 January 2012, 95–109.

Mignolo, Walter D., and Catherine E. Walsh. *On Decoloniality: Concepts, Analytics, Praxis*. Durham: Duke University Press, 2018.

2. From Black Studies to Afro-pessimism

Biondi, Martha. *The Black Revolution on Campus*. Berkeley: University of California Press, 2012.

Cruse, Harold, *The Crisis of the Negro Intellectual: A Historical Analysis of the Failure of Black Leadership*. New York: New York Review Books, 2005.

Wilderson, Frank B., III. *Incognegro: A Memoir of Exile and Apartheid*. Durham, NC: Duke University Press, 2015.

Patterson, Orlando. *Slavery and Social Death: A Comparative Study*. 1st Harvard University Press paperback ed. Cambridge, MA: Harvard University Press, 2018.

Warren, Calvin L. *Ontological Terror: Blackness, Nihilism, and Emancipation*. Durham, NC: Duke University Press, 2018.

Wilderson, Frank B. *Afropessimism*. New York: Liveright, 2021.

Hartman, Saidiya V. *Scenes of Subjection: Terror, Slavery, and Self-Making in Nineteenth-Century America*. Race and American Culture. New York: Oxford University Press, 1997.

Wekker, Gloria. 'Afropessimism'. *European Journal of Women's Studies*, 28:1, February 2021, 86–97.

Harney, Stefano, and Fred Moten. *All Incomplete*. Colchester: Minor Compositions, 2021.

Thomas, Greg. 'Afro-Blue Notes: The Death of Afro-pessimism (2.0)?'. *Theory and Event*, 21:1, 2018.

Olaloku-Teriba, Annie. 'Afro-Pessimism and the (Un)Logic of Anti-Blackness'. *Historical Materialism*, 26:2, 30 July 2018. 96–122.

3. Racial Capitalism and the Afterlives of Slavery

Robinson, Cedric J. *Black Marxism: The Making of the Black Radical Tradition*. London: Penguin Classics, 2021.

Williams, Eric. *Capitalism and Slavery*. 3rd ed. Chapel Hill: University of North Carolina Press, 2021.

Smallwood, Stephanie E. *Saltwater Slavery: A Middle Passage from Africa to American Diaspora*. Cambridge, MA: Harvard University Press, 2008.

Blackburn, Robin. *The Overthrow of Colonial Slavery 1776–1848*. London: Verso, 1988.

Hazareesingh, Sudhir. *Black Spartacus: The Epic Life of Toussaint Louverture*. London: Penguin Books, 2021.

Higginbottom, Andrew. 'Enslaved African Labour: Violent Racial Capitalism'. In *The Palgrave Encyclopedia of Imperialism and Anti-Imperialism*, edited by Immanuel Ness and Zak Cope, 1–16. Cham: Springer International Publishing, 2020.

Gonzalez, Johnhenry. *Maroon Nation: A History of Revolutionary Haiti*. Yale Agrarian Studies. New Haven: Yale University Press, 2019.

Dadzie, Stella. *A Kick in the Belly: Women, Slavery and Resistance*. London: Verso, 2021.

Keene, John. *Counternarratives*. New York: New Directions Books, 2015.

Silva, Denise Ferreira da. *Toward a Global Idea of Race*. Minneapolis: University of Minnesota Press, 2007.

4. Négritude and the (Mal)practice of Diaspora

Senghor, Léopold Sédar, and Jean-Paul Sartre. *Anthologie de la nouvelle poésie nègre et malgache de langue française*. 9th ed. Quadrige. Paris: PUF, 2015.

Diagne, Souleymane Bachir. *African Art as Philosophy: Senghor, Bergson, and the Idea of Negritude*. Translated by Chike Jeffers. Africa List. London: Seagull Books, 2011.

Césaire, Suzanne, and Daniel Maximin. *The Great Camouflage: Writings of Dissent (1941–1945)*. Translated by Keith L. Walker. 1st Wesleyan ed. Middletown, CT: Wesleyan University Press.

Césaire, Aimé, and Robin D.G. Kelley. *Discourse on Colonialism*. Translated by Joan Pinkham. New York: Monthly Review Press, 2000.

Spivak, Gayatri Chakravorty. *The Spivak Reader: Selected Works of Gayatri Chakravorty Spivak*. Edited by Donna Landry and Gerald MacLean. New York: Routledge, 1996.

Edwards, Brent Hayes. *The Practice of Diaspora: Literature, Translation, and the Rise of Black Internationalism*. Cambridge, MA: Harvard University Press, 2003.

Adi, Hakim. *Pan-Africanism: A History*. London: Bloomsbury Academic, 2018.

Younis, Musab. *On the Scale of the World: The Formation of Black Anticolonial Thought*. Oakland: University of California Press, 2022.

5. Whose Fanon? On Blackness and National Liberation

Fanon, Frantz. *Alienation and Freedom*. Edited by Jean Khalfa and Robert J.C. Young. Translated by Steven Corcoran. London: Bloomsbury Academic, 2018.

Fanon, Frantz. *Black Skin, White Masks*. Translated by Richard Philcox. New ed. New York: Grove Press, 2008.

Fanon, Frantz, and Jean-Paul Sartre. *The Wretched of the Earth*. Translated by Constance Farrington. Reprinted. London: Penguin Books, 2001.

Wynter, Sylvia. 'Human Being as Noun? Or Being Human as Praxis --Towards the Autopoetic Turn/Overturn: A Manifesto'. Unpublished paper. On *The Frantz Fanon Blog*, 27 October 2014, readingfanon.blogspot.com.

Gordon, Lewis Ricardo. *What Fanon Said: A Philosophical Introduction to His Life and Thought*. London: Hurst & Company, 2015.

Marriott, D.S. *Whither Fanon? Studies in the Blackness of Being*. Cultural Memory in the Present. Stanford, CA: Stanford University Press, 2018.

Smith, William Gardner, and Adam Shatz. *The Stone Face*. New York: New York Review Books, 2021.

6. Neo-colonialism, or, The Emptiness of Bearing One's Flag

Armah, Ayi Kwei. *The Beautyful Ones Are Not Yet Born*. African Writers Series. London: Heinemann, 2009.

Nkrumah, Kwame. *Neo-Colonialism: The Last Stage of Imperialism*, New York: International Publishers, 1976.

Mamdani, Mahmood. *Neither Settler nor Native: The Making and Unmaking of Permanent Minorities*. Cambridge, MA: Belknap Press of Harvard University Press, 2020.

Neocosmos, Michael. *Thinking Freedom in Africa: Toward a Theory of Emancipatory Politics*. Johannesburg: Wits University Press, 2016.

Wilson, Amrit. *The Threat of Liberation: Imperialism and Revolution in Zanzibar*. London: Pluto Press; 2013.

Condé, Maryse, and Richard Philcox. *What Is Africa to Me? Fragments of a True-to-Life Autobiography*. The Africa List. London: Seagull Books, 2017.

Rodney, Walter. *How Europe Underdeveloped Africa*. New ed. London: Verso, 2018.

Maloba, W.O. *The Anatomy of Neo-Colonialism in Kenya: British Imperialism and Kenyatta, 1963–1978*. London: Palgrave Macmillan, 2018.

Reza, Alexandra. 'I Write in Condé'. *London Review of Books*, 12 May 2022, lrb.co.uk.

7. Remnants of Red Africa

Mondlane, Eduardo. *The Struggle for Mozambique*. London: Zed Press, 1983.

Cabral, Amílcar, and Partido Africano da Independência da Guiné e Cabo Verde (PAIGC). *Unity and Struggle: Speeches and Writings*. New York: Monthly Review Press, 2016.

Cabral, Amílcar. *Return to the Source: Selected Speeches*. New York: Monthly Review Press, 1973/74.

Tomas, Antonio. *Amilcar Cabral: The Life of a Reluctant Nationalist*. London: C. Hurst & Co., 2019.

Telepneva, Natalia. *Cold War Liberation: The Soviet Union and the Collapse of the Portuguese Empire in Africa 1961–1975*. Chapel Hill: University of North Carolina Press, 2021.

Blouin, Andrée, and Jean Scott MacKellar. *My Country, Africa: Autobiography of the Black Pasionaria*. New York: Praeger Publishers, 1983.

Williams, Susan. *White Malice: The CIA and the Neocolonisation of Africa*. London: C Hurst & Co., 2021.

Jones, B.G. 'Anti-Racism and Emancipation in the Thought and Practice of Cabral, Neto, Mondlane and Machel'. In *International Relations and Non-Western Thought*, edited by R. Shilliam, 47-63. Abingdon: Routledge, 2011.

Rabaka, R. *Concepts of Cabralism: Amilcar Cabral and Africana Critical Theory*. 1st ed. London: Lexington Books, 2014.

Afterword

Amin, Samir. *Modern Imperialism, Monopoly Finance Capital, and Marx's Law of Value*. New York: Monthly Review Press, 2018.

Smith, John Charles. *Imperialism in the Twenty-First Century: Globalization, Super-Exploitation, and Capitalism's Final Crisis*. New York: Monthly Review Press, 2016.

Latimer, Amanda, 'Super-Exploitation, the Race to the Bottom, and the Missing International'. In *The Palgrave Encyclopedia of Imperialism and Anti-Imperialism*, edited by Immanuel Ness and Zak Cope. Cham: Springer International Publishing, 2020.

Rodney, Walter. *Decolonial Marxism: Essays from the Pan-African Revolution*. London: Verso, 2022.

Selwyn, Daniel. *Martial Mining*. London: London Mining Network, 2020.